DOUBLE EXPOSURE

DOUBLE EXPOSURE

EP Thompson

The Merlin Press
LONDON

First Published in 1985 by
The Merlin Press
3 Manchester Road
Isle of Dogs
London E14

British Library Cataloguing in Publication Data

Thompson, E.P.
Double exposure.
1. Thompson, E.P. 2. Historians—Great Britain
—Biography 3. Antinuclear movement—Great
Britain—History
I. Title
327.1'72'0924 D15.T5/

ISBN 0-85036-333-0

Cover design by Louis MacKay

Typesetting by Hems and Co.
The Old Brewery
Tisbury, Wilts. SP3 6NH

Printed by Whitstable Litho
Millstrood Road,
Whitstable, Kent

CONTENTS

To

Zdena Tomin

INTRODUCTION

In the last months of 1984, when I was preparing a collection called *The Heavy Dancers* for the press, it occurred to me that some of the matters discussed in those pages concealed a 'hidden narrative' of the non-aligned peace movement of the past five years.

This narrative has been hidden simply because the actors have been too busy to write it. It concerns the origins of a part of that movement; the increasingly sharp attacks (and calumnies) visited upon it by orthodox Western critics; the co-operation between Western peace movements and independent peace groups in the East; and the sharp and confrontational response to this from official sources in the Communist apparatus.

While some part of this record is known to many active members of Western peace movements, only a few hundred people have been centrally involved in these events. It seemed to be time to make the record more public. But when I sat down to write an introduction to *The Heavy Dancers*, it turned out that matters were too complex to despatch in a few pages. My fingers became trapped in my typewriter for weeks.

This essay is the result. It is a companion to *The Heavy Dancers*, but it is also a distinct study in itself and one which is addressed in particular to persons active in the peace movement. It is not offered as an objective narrative of the past five years. No-one is competent to write that yet, and it would require research into numerous national histories and movements. Yet, since something needed to be written, I decided to write this in a more personal way. Because I have exposed my views often in publication, I have drawn upon myself numerous attacks, some of a quite personal nature. Most of them have been too trivial or too bigoted to answer; yet replying to some of them has given me a gate-of-entry into general questions of history and of ideology of more public interest.

There is also the difficulty that a writer cannot always (without some auto-suppression) argue out difficult points as a representative of some collectivity: a Campaign or a Committee. Political, moral, and philosphical matters raised here are not ones as to which organisations have 'positions'. The positions are my own. And, where narrative enters in, I have also drawn directly on my own personal experience. No doubt in that part of this essay which considers East/West relations, a much fuller (and richer) account could be given by those who have had direct experience of Soviet, Polish, GDR or Czechoslovak exchanges. But in keeping with the manner of this essay I have confined my examples to matters which came most directly within my own observation.

This essay therefore should not be taken as expressing the views of 'the peace movement' or of CND or END. But it could not have been written without their collective work and experience. This is so much the case that it is impossible to single out individuals for acknowledgement—and a few of them, on 'the other side', might not thank me for doing so. I will only say that I owe most of all to my colleagues in the British Committee of END (European Nuclear Disarmament), and, in the second half of this essay, to those specialist groups of END which have made it their work to monitor developments and to communicate with citizens on 'the other side'. Some passages of Chapter Five have appeared in *END Journal* (October 1984) and in a fuller essay on 'Star Wars' in the *Guardian*, 18 February 1985.

Worcester E.P.T.
January 1985

I 'A HANDFUL OF SCOUNDRELS'

On April 25th, 1983, General Bernard Rogers, the Supreme Allied Commander, NATO, was giving evidence before the House of Representatives Committee on Armed Services, Procurement and Military Nuclear Systems in Washington. A major argument against the freeze movement in the United States (he said),

> . . . is the support that the freeze gives to those movements in Western Europe that are counterproductive to our efforts, because they look back and they say, 'look at what's going on in the United States, we have got support there'. It plays right into the hands of a man named Thompson, who heads the campaign for nuclear disarmament in the U.K., who has come out and said as much. Just the fact that you are considering such a freeze, you see, plays into his hands.

It is flattering to know that I have come to the notice of someone so eminent as General Rogers, although it suggests an alarming state of incompetence in NATO's intelligence services that they have not yet been able to identify who 'heads' CND. And I was equally flattered to learn a few months later that I had also come to the notice of Mr Georgi Arbatov, the director of Moscow's Institute of US and Canadian Studies. In private discussions with both Dutch and Belgian peace workers, in the summer of 1983, he referred to me and to END (European Nuclear Disarmament) somewhat curtly as 'affairs of the CIA'.

It is not only General Rogers and Mr Arbatov to whom I have given offence. I have had, in 1983 and 1984, a sensationally bad press from ideologists on both sides of the Cold War: from *Encounter* and *Commentary* (which both come from stables which, in the first Cold War, received laundered subventions from the CIA—although, in the case of *Encounter*, the torch of subvention was later handed on to the British Arts Council); and from such journals as *Rude Pravo*, *Pravda* and *International Life* in the East. For an advocate of peace, and of a healing-process between the blocs, this is discouraging. Indeed, I have been the target of so much abuse that I have often thought that it would most contribute to the peace of the world, as well as to my own peace-of-mind, if I just shut up.

Yet at a time when the superpowers can agree on almost nothing, I and some of my friends have at least provided them with a common bond. If the Geneva negotiations had been, not about cruise, Pershing and SS-20s but about how to rub out the non-aligned peace movements (including 'a man named Thompson') then the negotiators would have come out smiling and arm-in-arm.

I suppose that I do really know what makes both lots of them so cross. First, it is essential to their world-view (and to their arms procurements) that they should uphold a binary, Us-versus-Them, definition of world politics. The very notion that there might be alternative ways is threatening to them both. Second, neither lot likes being called the 'ideological look-alikes' of the other. This is deeply wounding to their self-esteem. It might also give the game away—a game in which they are partners as well as antagonists.

The Heavy Dancers chronicles these complex arguments between peace movements and the war movement—and it may be helpful to explain something of their context. One way of doing this may be to comment on my critics.

From the West one kind of criticism falls into the category which I will define as 'political soft porn': that is, it makes no pretence of confronting my arguments but ransacks my writings over thirty and more years, pulling the odd sentence or phrase out of context, and uses these to flash lubricious signals suggestive of devious motives and of disguised complicity with Soviet strategies.

Since I am known as a vocal critic of official Soviet ideology and power, they hint that this is only a rhetorical device to make me the more persuasive as the proponent of a peace movement whose objective effect (if successful) would be to disarm 'the West' unilaterally and expose it to Soviet occupation or blackmail. It is left to readers to decide whether I am 'disingenuous' and a 'dangerous' undercover Soviet agent or merely 'self-deluded'.

In this category of political soft porn fall 'Portrait of a Peace-Fighter' by Gerald Frost in *Encounter*, May 1984, and 'The "Neutralism" of E.P. Thompson' by Scott McConnell in *Commentary* in the summer of 1983. Mr Frost is attributed with the high-sounding title of Executive Director of the Institute for European Defence and Strategic Studies, an 'Institute' with which Mr Roger Scruton is also associated but which turns out to be, not an academic foundation, but a private office in London. I have already replied to Mr Frost's scatter-shot (*Encounter*, 'Letters', July/August 1984). An example of Mr McConnell's technique (which verges on the political hard porn) may be taken to exemplify his method.

I counted some twenty-seven direct mis-statements or direct mis-representations in McConnell's seven pages; here is a characteristic example. McConnell is commenting on the fact that my central preoccupations changed in late 1979, 'in the aftermath of the NATO decision to deploy cruise and Pershing missiles':

> One need not speculate on the particular events which prompted the change. It is true that Thompson focused his concern on the campaign for unilateral disarmament right after returning from a visit to Bulgaria, in the fall of 1979, where preparations were just beginning for the Soviet-sponsored World Peace Council festival, planned for Sofia the following year (preparations which, it has been noted, followed directly upon the Soviet decision to invade Afghanistan). But Thompson did, after all, have personal reasons for his visit (his brother died in Bulgaria during the war). Moreover, he had not been a party man for some time, and he was certainly

> **able to conceive of the significance of the peace issue without higher guidance.**

The intention of this passage is to discount the actual reasons for my active involvement in the peace movement in those months—the failure of the USA to ratify SALT II, the NATO modernisation decisions, and the Soviet invasion of Afghanistan were leading on to a dangerous bloc confrontation—reasons which were clearly stated by me in articles in *New Society*, the *Guardian* and the *New Statesman* at the time. The passage insinuates that there must have been ulterior reasons, which might be deduced—if all were known—from his muddy passage about Bulgaria. The suggestion is made that I might (or, again, I might not) have received Soviet 'guidance' during this visit, and this suggestion is allowed to linger in the mind although it is, as proof of McConnell's fair-mindedness, then partially withdrawn. Since I had not been 'a party man for some time' (in fact I had left the Communist Party in 1956, twenty-three years before) I might have fallen within these Soviet guide-lines of my own accord. (McConnell had already prepared for this expectation by describing me as 'a sort of fellow-traveller with his own car'). What is left behind with the reader is the sense that something malodorous was going on.

The stench, however, comes from McConnell's own insinuations, which entail a direct inversion of historical sequence. I visited Bulgaria with my wife, Dorothy, not 'in the fall' but in April 1979; we went as private tourists, although on the invitation of the association of former partisans of World War II. We were collecting information both in South Serbia and Bulgaria, about my brother's part as a British Liaison Officer (SOE) with the partisans, in which he met his death; and in due course I hope to publish a study of this odd corner of that war.

Our relations with the Bulgarian authorities were courteous but formal and were exclusively related to this question. I had never heard of cruise missiles or of NATO modernisation at that time. I do not remember hearing of the World Peace Council event in Sofia (which took place eighteen months later) until after it had happened. Moreover, McConnell engages in extraordinary acrobatics in suggesting that 'preparations' for the Sofia event were taking place 'in the fall' of 1979 as a result of the Soviet invasion of Afghanistan, which took place in December 1979, two weeks *after* the NATO modernisation decision of December 12th. The actual historical sequence (our visit to Bulgaria, April 1979; NATO modernisation decision, December 12, 1979, Soviet invasion of Afghanistan, December 26, 1979; Sofia World Peace Council conference, September 1980) is inverted to insinuate that I received 'higher guidance' from the organisers of a conference (at which I was not present and to which I was not invited) which took place 18 months after our visit.

To plant a libel by both offering it and disclaiming it is a well-known technique of this kind of porn. But McConnell is also suggesting an extraordinary conspiracy-theory of politics. 'Preparations' for the Sofia conference 'it has been noted, followed directly upon the Soviet decision to invade Afghanistan'. The far-sighted engineers of Soviet subversion (it seems) had already decided to invade Afghanistan (when? in September 1979? or in April, when I was in Sofia?) and were already winding-up the master-spring of the European and American peace movements of the future. And this conspiracy has 'already been noted'. Where? By whom?

I think that in this case I can provide the answer. Vladimir Bukovsky had already published in *Commentary* in 1982 his long article, *The Peace Movement and the Soviet Union*, which was then republished in England, first in *The Times*, and then, with an introduction by Winston S. Churchill, MP, as a pamphlet promoted by the Coalition for Peace through Security. It was also published in Holland, Germany, and no doubt in other countries. The French edition, *Les pacifistes contre la paix*, was a sensational success, and week after week Bukovsky could be read pontificating on Soviet strategy and on the peace movement in such intellectual organs as *Paris Match*. I think it possible that Bukovsky's accusations that the peace movement was the creature of Soviet agencies had an influence upon delaying the development of an independent French movement.

Vladimir Bukovsky is a Soviet 'dissident' who was treated ferociously by the KGB and who, after long terms of imprisonment and of forcible commitment to psychiatric institutes was finally deported to the West (in a celebrated 'exchange' with the Chilean Communist leader, Luis Corvalan) in 1976. His experiences have been savage, and were endured with stoicism, and they entitle him to deploy some verbal savagery in arguments with opponents. Indeed, if he were testifying on matters within his direct experience, I could only attend to his testimony with humility.

He has however offered testimony on a great many other matters which lie far outside his experience. In the West he has bounced back like a rubber ball and he is full of ebullience. He enjoys the theatre of things, especially when he is centre-stage, and he has a charming way of gesturing, exaggerating for effect, and saying whatever comes into his head. He published in Paris in 1981 *Cette lancinante douleur de la liberté* (This Agonising Pain of Liberty), subtitled 'Letters of a Russian resister to Westerners', in which he chronicled the agonies, comedies and errors of finding his way in the Free West—mainly in England. It is clear that the Free West has not lived up to his expectations; we have disappointed him; the British did not let him bring in his dog from Switzerland since they were firmly persuaded that madness in animals comes from abroad and 'any island madness is quite unthinkable'.

In short, he takes the mickey out of us, it is good fun, and he has some perceptive comments as well. His style strives for effect, not for veracity. Contrasting the serious reading-habits of the average Soviet citizen with the English, he writes that 'when in 1978 I was looking for lodgings in Cambridge, I visited a hundred houses and I practically never saw any books except for telephone directories'. I can well believe the contrast, but I cannot believe that he really went to 100 houses looking for digs nor that almost none of them had any books.

I can suppose that if he had not crossed me in other ways I would have enjoyed an evening with Bukovsky, over a bottle of wine, sounding off irresponsibly about everything under the sun. But there are some matters one cannot be irresponsible about. In these same letters he was so irresponsible—for example, in an ill-based attack on Roy Medvedev and on his fellow-expatriate, Dr Zhores Medvedev—that publishers thought it prudent not to risk an English edition.

This careless disregard for veracity, this gesturing for effect, combined with a pretence to omniscience as to Soviet conspiracy and subterfuge, are the hallmarks of *The Peace Movement and the Soviet Union*. This tract does not offer very much, proves even less, but insinuates a great deal. He shouts at the top of his voice that the British peace movement and CND have said nothing (or 'only in whispers') about Soviet SS-20s, and 'proves' this by citing a pamphlet by Betty England. But the widest-selling pamphlet of 1980, co-published by CND, was my own *Protest and Survive* (subsequently a Penguin Collection, edited by Dan Smith and myself), and these have sufficient to say about SS-20s. Bukovsky, who was then studying at Cambridge, should have had no difficulty in reading these. He did not wish to do so, any more than he wished to hear those voices in the peace movement which were raised on behalf of Dr Sakharov: 'during all the time that hundreds of thousands of "peace-lovers" were noisily expressing their one-sided feelings on the streets of London, Bonn, Amsterdam and Brussels, not one word was said about Sakharov. . .' This also is untrue; many words have been said by many voices, and I recall especially the first great peace demonstration in Bonn on October 10th, 1981, and the great surge of applause in the immense attentive crowd when the novelist, Heinrich Böll, referred in moving terms to Sakharov as his friend.*

* Böll's speech is in *Bonn 10.10.1981* (Lamuv Verlag, 1981), p. 161. Support in the Western peace movement for Dr Sakharov diminished after his open letter (published in *Foreign Affairs* in 1983) which appeared to support NATO modernisation on grounds of 'balance'. In my own view, Dr Sakharov, in his exile at Gorky, has access to only partial information: and the blame for this rests wholly upon the Soviet authorities. Western peace movements should request that they might visit Dr Sakharov, receive his views, and bring him relevant peace research materials.

But Bukovsky does not wish to know. He does not suggest that rational debate is permissible. He knows everything already, without the trouble of finding out. He knows that the World Peace Council campaign of the early 1950s (the Stockholm Appeal and the rest) was 'organized, conducted, and financed from Moscow'—and I think that in some part it was—and therefore it must follow that the campaigns of the past four years must be exactly the same. He required no evidence to know that the new peace movement was 'a Soviet booby-trap': 'I make no claim to special prescience; it is just that after 34 years in my beloved Communist motherland, I have some sense of its government's bag of tricks, pranks and stunts.' And, on the basis of this insight, he is able to categorise the Western peace movement of today:

> Just as it did in the 1950s, the movement today probably consists of the same odd mixture of Communists, fellow-travellers, muddle-headed intellectuals, hypocrites seeking popularity, professional political speculators, frightened bourgeois, and youths eager to rebel just for the sake of rebelling. There are also the inevitable Catholic priests with a 'mission' and other religious people who believe that God has chosen them to make peace on earth right now. But there is also not the slightest doubt that this motley crowd is manipulated by a handful of scoundrels instructed directly from Moscow.

That is fairly strong stuff. It went down well not only with Winston S. Churchill (who has the same knockabout polemical style and the same impatience with veracity) but with the readers of the *Daily Telegraph* and the *Daily Mail*. But it falls a little short of proof: 'not the slightest doubt. . . manipulated by scoundrels. . . directly from Moscow'—and how do we know? The proof, if any, was offered in a *virtuoso* passage in which Bukovsky discovered that the whole movement had been set in motion by the 'World Parliament of the Peoples for Peace', organised by the World Peace Council in Sofia, in September 1980. Not only this: Bukovsky also finds in *Pravda* an interview with an organiser of this event, who reveals that 'preparations' for it began 'about a year earlier'. But, shouts Bukovsky, a year earlier, in September 1979, 'the sky was cloudless'. 'There was no new escalation in the arms race. . . The Vienna summit meeting had just been successfully concluded with the signing of SALT II.' *Ergo:* the Soviet leaders must have already decided to invade Afghanistan, and with remarkable forethought set in motion at the same time a future Western peace movement to soften the future consequences.

I have met with this kind of ideological history, in which the actual events are contorted or inverted in order to encode the correct ideological message, fairly often from Soviet bloc apologists, but it is sad to see Bukovsky at the same trade. Bukovsky pretends to have tracked down 'the earliest traces' of the peace movement's revival to this Sofia event, and McConnell follows on in *Commentary* by taking Bukovsky's fiction for established fact. We have at least tracked down that source.

I have one qualification for discussing the 'earliest traces' of the revival of the movement which is denied to Bukovsky and McConnell: I was myself an 'earliest trace' and I was deeply involved in its formation. I do not intend to write this history, although its evidences still lie about me in my files or on my floor. But it should be noted, first, that the Sofia 'Parliament' had almost no influence on the generation of the Western movement (I do not recall it even being discussed), and, second, that many of that movement's key elements were active long before that event.

These elements owed little or nothing to 'Moscow', and most of them were strictly non-aligned. In Holland the crucially-influential IKV, or Interchurch Peace Council, funded by the major churches, was long-established, had a small expert staff, and also (which is more important than some peace activists suppose) had got ahead with its *thinking:* it had developed theories (which it continues to develop) of the principles of non-alignment, of East–West relations and of relations between North and South. It had campaigned with effect, alongside the Dutch 'No to Neutron Weapons' (at that time under some Communist influence) against the neutron bomb, as had also the non-aligned Norwegian movement. In Europe as a whole there were several networks of small non-aligned peace organisations: the International Confederation for Disarmament and Peace, with which Peggy Duff (the first General Secretary of CND) was associated, and which had had its own traumatic history maintaining independence from the World Peace Council: the International Peace Bureau: the War Resisters International: the Fellowship of Reconciliation: and others. (These organisations also had affiliates in the United States, Japan and Australia.) There were also substantial political forces searching for some alternative to the blocs, not least among them influential sections of Labour and Social-Democratic parties and those Eurocommunists in Italy and Spain whose first principle was *not* to be 'instructed directly from Moscow'.

In Britain, where most of these elements could be found, CND had declined over the previous decade to pitifully small numbers. But it still existed, in January 1980, was experiencing a revival, and had the great good fortune to find as General Secretary Bruce Kent. At that same moment a group of us (which included Bruce Kent and Peggy Duff) began meeting and corresponding with a view to launching a movement to clear all nuclear weapons out of Europe. The proposal was first made by Ken Coates. I drafted the original Appeal, which was then redrafted and revised by several hands, including Ken Coates, Mary Kaldor, Dan Smith, Dorothy Thompson, and with some advice from Claude Bourdet in Paris, Ulrich Albrecht in Berlin, Dr. Zhores Medvedev and others. The END Appeal was as clear a statement of non-aligned perspectives as we could make it, and as such it still stands as the charter-document of three major Conventions of the European peace movements (Brussels, 1982; Berlin, 1983; Perugia, 1984):

> We must resist any attempt by the statesmen of East or West to manipulate this movement to their own advantage. We offer no advantage to either NATO or the Warsaw alliance. Our objectives must be to free Europe from confrontation, to enforce detente between the United States and the Soviet Union, and, ultimately, to dissolve both great power alliances.

From February 1980 onwards the work of collecting signatures to the Appeal went forward, under the energetic direction, not of Moscow, but of the Bertrand Russell Peace Foundation, an office in Nottingham with wide experience and international connections and with a record on 'human rights' which had often got up Moscow's nose. Both before and after April (when the Appeal was formally published) thousands of European signatures were collected, including those of prominent intellectuals, politicians and trade-unionists over a wide spectrum of opinion. And with the collection, European and then transatlantic networking increased.

This was an important contribution to the revival of the European peace movement and to its new form. It was, of course, only one contribution. The Dutch IKV, which was scarcely known to us then, was building its own network. Other groups were reaching outwards: the Greens in West Germany: the *Il Manifesto* group in Italy: women's networks: the older bodies and alliances which I have mentioned: and, on both sides of the Atlantic, the Quakers.*

In this thumbnail impression I mean only to emphasise that a complex social movement is made up of many elements, just as a great river is fed by many streams, and that the conspiracy theory favoured by Messrs Bukovsky, Churchill, McConnell and Frost is not only false but is absurd. All this had long been on the road, in 1980, before that Sofia conference (which none of us attended). Among the influential writings being discussed in Britain in 1980 (long before the World Peace Council resolutions which Bukovsky cites) were Lord Mountbatten's famous speech, articles by Lord Zuckerman and George Kennan and the Penguin collection, *Protest and Survive*, none of which were

* Diana Johnstone's *The Politics of Euromissiles* (Verso, 1984) gives valuable background to the development of the peace movement, less from the viewpoint of the kitchen (where we peace activists were sweating at the stove) than from that of the parlours where higher politics went on. Her treatment of Germany, Italy and Belgium is especially helpful, but her view of Holland, Britain and Scandinavia suffers from Parisian myopia. See also Ken Coates, *The Most Dangerous Decade* (Spokesman, 1984).

drafted in Moscow.

The West German movement developed more slowly, and Bukovsky will have it that the Bonn demonstration of October 1981 was set up in Sofia the year before. There was a little external influence upon Germany, of which I have poignant recollections. For in March 1981 the END Committee in Britain, on the initiative of Peggy Duff and Bruce Kent, called a small conference of European peace activists in Frankfurt.

This was Peggy's last conference, and it was, very much, her conference. She had used all her experience, and the network of the non-aligned ICDP, to bring the delegates together. It was at this conference that I first met many peace workers who have since become firm friends or allies, including Ilkka Taipale of the Finnish Peace Union, Gynt Krag of the Norwegian 'No to Nuclear Weapons', and Eva Quistorp of West German Women for Peace.

I travelled both ways with Peggy. She was riddled with cancer, and used a stick or a wheel-chair. We arrived very early at Frankfurt because of a cheap air ticket (none of the 'astronomical' Soviet subsidies which Bukovsky reports ever reached us) and went to the Spartan youth hostel which was not ready to receive us. I managed to get a room where Peggy could lie on a bunk: she had nothing to eat all day but a carton of milk. Then the first delegates started to arrive. I did not know whether to disturb Peggy, but she had ordered me to do so and (since we were all a little scared of her) I did. She hobbled down the passage, and as she saw her old (and new) friends assembling, an amazing power of the spirit seemed to lighten her eyes and to assume command over her for the next three days. It was a successful conference, and it was Peggy who chaired the final session, making sure that the talk ended in clear decisions. We travelled back together the next day, and we had time to talk over many things, including her many conflicts with the World Peace Council and 'the Russians'.

Peggy died within two months and we have missed her advice grievously ever since. I have put this down because, when I recall the kind of commitment which her life embodied, then the Bukovsky-McConnell-type fictions rise in my gorge. I will not claim that the Frankfurt END conference was the starter-motor of the West German movement. It was just one kick on that motor. And there were plenty of kicks in Germany itself. We had seven or eight different groups of West German activists present (women, war resisters, Easter marchers, Peace Society, supporters of the Krefeld Appeal, Rudolph Bahro from the Greens), who, at the end of the conference, met together for the first time and made plans. At about the same time the Dutch IKV was exerting its influence also, especially among the Protestant churches. The first real signal that the German movement had arrived was at the Protestant Church Day in Hamburg that June. Then came the amazing October demonstration in Bonn, whose youthfulness, good-humour and restraint seemed to signal a mutation in German culture, and whose formidable platform—General Bastian, Petra Kelly, Erhard Eppler, Heinrich Böll and also (please remember) Coretta King—could scarcely be described as 'a handful of scoundrels instructed directly from Moscow'.

For all that I know Bukovsky may really believe what he writes. As he says himself in his tract, 'sometimes it is very comfortable—even for professional intellectuals—not to know things. . .' But that does not excuse him of irresponsibility, in not trying to find out. I do not mean that there has been no pro-Moscow Communist influence in the Western peace movement. On the contrary, there has been, and there continues to be, and some of it does come directly from Moscow; it has been damaging and time-wasting and we will deal with it anon. In West Germany, for example, the influential Krefeld Appeal against NATO missiles was silent about Soviet weapons; it was backed by an alliance which included both the non-aligned Greens (Bastian and Kelly) and the DKP (German Communist Party)—an alliance which came under increasing strain until it fell apart. In other countries there have been splits between pro-Moscow and non-aligned movements: France, Denmark, Finland, Greece.

What I mean is that Bukovsky and his followers present the movements as a coarse lampoon and in crucial ways they invert the true history. The new peace movement was never a replay of the World Peace Council campaign of the Fifties. It discovered itself, from a multitude of sources, and from small non-aligned bases established in the previous decades (ICDP, IPB, Russell Foundation, IKV, CND, War Resisters). It was moving powerfully in Britain, Scandinavia, Holland and Belgium before whatever went on in Sofia, and from that time on the World Peace Council has been panting after it, trying to catch hold of its coat-tails and to claim it as its own.

Bukovsky's lampoon has been damaging to us, perhaps in France and perhaps also in those places in Eastern Europe where *Commentary* and *Encounter* are assiduously read, precisely because it serves to confirm and to enforce exactly the same ideological fiction which the Communist ideologues wish to impose: that the *true* peace movement is, or ought to be, the compliant ally of peace-loving Soviet diplomacy in the face of imperialist aggression, and that the non-aligned forces (who in fact started it off and who represent its major movements) are late-comers and 'infiltrators' of 'NATO agencies'.

The Cold War world is a merciless world and it sets these cruel traps for us all. But there are some of us who scarcely deserved this treatment at Bukovsky's hands. For, looking through old files, I notice a press release of the Bertrand Russell Peace Foundation in 1974. In this, there is an announcement of a series of Days of Protest on behalf of civil rights prisoners in Eastern Europe, and especially in the USSR and Czechoslovakia, called jointly by the Russell Foundation, Pavel Litvinov, Jiri Pelikan and Andrei Sakharov. General Grigorenko was to be the theme of protest on the first day (7 May 1974), Jaroslav Šabata and Jiri Muller of Czechoslovakia on the second day (27 November 1974), and on the third Day of Protest (29 March 1975)—Vladimir Bukovsky! And I also notice, in a letter from Ken Coates to the *Times Literary Supplement* (November 22, 1974) that I was one of the platform speakers at the meeting at Conway Hall for Šabata and Muller; and that a number of persons subsequently prominent in the revival of the peace movement (including Noam Chomsky, Daniel Ellsberg,

Christopher Hill and myself) were signatories to the general appeal. So far as I can remember I spoke on Bukovsky Day also, on a university campus, and very certainly the Russell Peace Foundation continued its work for our impatient author.

So that it turns out that Vladimir Bukovsky has lampooned as 'useful idiots' directly 'controlled from Moscow' a Foundation and individuals which both campaigned for his own release and which played a major role in launching the Appeal for a nuclear-free Europe. I am not making any complaint about 'ingratitude'. Those of us on the 'Left' in the past three decades who have busied ourselves with issues of human rights in Communist countries have got used to finding out that the first thing that certain 'dissidents' do when they get to the West is slap us across the face with a wet fish. Yet the question of civil rights is not a question of political trading; it is an absolute; we do not defend these prisoners because they will say what we want them to say but because they have the right to say what they want themselves. We do not lay upon anyone a debt of gratitude because we do what is our plain duty.

Direct East-West communication now is like a faint exchange on the radio against a mass of static and with the jamming of the ideologists of both sides. Yet now and then a message *does* get through, and these are moments without price. It is heartening to know that, in 1974, some of us held a Day of Protest for Jaroslav Šabata—a protest he may not have known about in his prison and may not know about today. Yet today his voice has come back to us, loud and clear through the static, in his remarkable letter to the peace movement in *Voices from Prague*.

We have drifted a long way from Messrs Frost and McConnell and it would be a drag to go back to them. What they are chiefly interested in doing, with respect to myself, is to flash upon the anxious reader's mind the fact that I was a member of the Communist Party as a young man (between 1942 and 1956) and to suggest that I have never been sufficiently penitent about this and therefore should be suspect as a possible accomplice of 'Moscow'.* The difficulty in meeting this kind of attack, which is mounted not against my arguments but against my own credibility, is that it can be answered only by going off into autobiography or apologia. I would have to dive into page after page of personal matters, and chew over once more the issues of thirty years ago—questions which have nothing to do with today's peace movement and the positions which we hold in common. I am damned if I can see why any of my colleagues in today's movement should feel bound to endorse my whole life's history, any more than I feel bound to endorse theirs.

I have written out, over the years, at inordinate length my own reflections on the whole Communist and ex-Communist experience, in the *Reasoner*, the *New Reasoner*, *The Poverty of Theory*, and elsewhere. It is true that I have not, and still do not, repent of everything that I did as a Communist between 1942 and 1956. After I had finished being a soldier (which I do not repent) my main political preoccupation was in work for peace. We opposed a series of almost forgotten wars (in Greece, Algeria, Malaya, Cyprus, and Kenya), and I served as Secretary of the Federation of West Yorkshire Peace Organisations and as editor of our occasional journal, the *Yorkshire Voice of Peace*, at the height of the Korean War and during the run-up to German re-armament. All these actions still seem to me to have been right and necessary. At the same time, as I have often written, the Communist apologetics for Stalin's Russia were grossly dishonest and self-deluding, entailed direct betrayals of principle and of persons, and the whole international (World Peace Council) and sometimes national framework into which our authentic grass-roots peace movement was slotted was manipulated—in the last resort from 'Moscow'.

When all this has been said, on both sides, there is still one question remaining: which is, 'What, in those years, was

* Heseltine flashed in the same way in the run-up to the General Election in 1983, employing the resources of a special section of the MOD to research the political biographies of members of CND Council and passing on the findings to the *Express*. Some civil servants thought his employment of public resources upon party-political porn to be an unconstitutional abuse.

the right and effective course of political action?' It may not be difficult to suggest theoretically 'correct' positions, such as those of the Fourth or Seventh International, or, perhaps, suicide. It is a good deal more difficult to suggest how anyone might have acted with *effect.* As NATO and the Warsaw Pact were set up against each other, the world (and certainly Europe) was divided not only in theory but in fact into Two Camps. And as more state papers are opened it is clear that on occasions the 'nuclear option' was certainly considered by the United States: very certainly during the Korean War. In Britain it may be forgotten how unreservedly Labour's leaders were committed to NATO and the American alliance; there was no tolerance in the Labour Party towards third ways. I think that we had no alternative to work for peace in the ways that we did, simply because there was no political space in which an alternative could then be pressed with effect.

That is a pragmatic point, not a theoretical excuse. I was not then looking for that alternative space, although I can now see, in retrospect, that a few were trying to hold it open: perhaps A.J. Muste and I.F. Stone in America, Claude Bourdet in France, in Britain G.D.H. Cole. The space did not open until after Stalin's death and the Khrushchev 'thaw'. In 1956 there was a world-wide effort of internal Communist 'revision' or reform, both in the East (Poland, the Soviet Union itself, Hungary) and in Western parties. When this was checked within the old ideological and disciplinary norms, many thousands of Communists (of whom I was one) left their parties, and many of these sought to break open that alternative space. Many gave support to CND and to the new non-aligned peace movements of that generation. Some survivors from that moment are among the elements who put together the peace movement of today.

But this recantation and redirection falls far short of what is required by the sages of *Encounter* and *Commentary.* They would be satisfied with nothing less than abject apostasy. Rehabilitation requires that we should proclaim the whole of 'Communism' a contaminated area and call down an anathema upon all its works. It is my offence, in the eyes of Mr Frost and Mr McConnell that I have steadfastly refused to do this. I have polemicised against Marxism as ideology, but I have not disowned my debt to an open, innovative Marxist tradition. I have pronounced my anathemas upon Communist statism—and the mental controls and all-intrusive and brutal security measures of the present Soviet regime are beyond reach of any apology—but I have also noted contradictory (and potentially democratic) elements in the Communist inheritance, the capacity of some Communist-ruled societies for some measure of self-reform (Prague, 1968), and even for more dramatic popular renewal (Poland and Solidarnosc).

Indeed, it is exactly within the contradiction between repressive form and human potential in Communist societies that one of the hopes for human survival may be found. If one does not see a potential for internal transformation, what future can a dedicated anti-Communist offer? What future (let us say) can M. André Glucksmann offer? He can offer only to pile up more and more 'deterrents', in a delicious state of vertigo, in the hope that in some future all Communists and all their rabbits will die. That is the mentality of war, the mentality of abstract and ideologically-obsessed anti-Communism.

But I see around us all the time the evidences of Communist contradiction. There has never been a time when official Soviet ideology and the commonsense of lived Soviet experience were more at odds than they are today. The ideology of 'actually existing Socialism' is nothing but patches and holes. Outside the Warsaw powers bloc we observe all the variants of Eurocommunism. Visiting the peace movement in Barcelona in 1984 I was struck by the vigorous contribution to it made by members and ex-members of the Catalan CP (mainly ex); Spanish Communists, who suffered under Franco and whose party was brutally treated by Stalin, know a thing or two about human rights. They expressed the hope that one of the effects of a non-aligned peace movement would be to offer alliances with Solidarnosc and with Charter 77, and to assist forward the

Communist world's democratic self-transformation. And who will they be assisting? Some of those courageous spokespersons of human rights who are now making their voices heard by the Western peace movement through the ideological static (for example, Ladislav Lis and Jaroslav Šabata) are themselves—former Communists.

The world is not so tidy as M. Glucksmann or as *Commentary* suppose. Nor is it as abstract. I do not argue any special privilege for ex-Communists in the peace movement. It is significant that Mr George Kennan, who was of the opposite party during the first Cold War, is now an ex-*anti*-Communist and has come to the same conclusions from the other side. But if we are to heal this broken world, and introduce the forces making for peace and for democracy on both sides to each other, then ex-Communists and Eurocommunists (as well as ex-anti-Communists) have their role within that healing-process. And it may not be unhelpful to the peace movement to have among its members some persons who have learned, from sad experience, about both the 'tricks, pranks and stunts' of the Communist Party bureaucrats and about the contradictions between Communist forms and potentials.

II 'MORAL ENDS' AND AMERICA'S 'MISSION'

It is a relief to turn aside from Messrs Frost, Bukovsky and McConnell and to turn to a writer who attends in earnest to arguments. Mr Leon Wieseltier wrote a long essay in the *New Republic* (January 10 & 17, 1983) which was then put out as a book, *Nuclear War, Nuclear Peace*. This was very warmly received by the United States establishment, including Dr Henry Kissinger and ('a masterwork') Senator Daniel Moynihan. Wieseltier's strategy is to set up a 'Party of Peace' on one side (Jonathan Schell, George Kennan and myself) and a 'Party of War' on the other side (Colin Gray, Edward Luttwack and others), to expose both parties as extremist, and then to hew a 'moderate' path between them in which he vindicates the theories of 'deterrence', moderated by superpower arms control. Wieseltier occupies that part of the 'moderate' spectrum in the United States that Professor Lawrence Freedman occupies in Britain: in short, he is very much in favour of NATO modernisation, Trident II, and other such measures to 'maintain deterrence', but he criticises certain excesses of NATO strategists in order to sustain an image of 'moderation'.

The rehabilitation of 'deterrence' is a booming industry on both sides of the Atlantic. It is agreed that nuclear war would be an unthinkable disaster; therefore we must strengthen 'deterrence', which is the only way to avoid it; to prevent nuclear war we must procure more nuclear weapons. What is surprising is that some of this rehabilitation has gone on in the *New York Review of Books*, where, alongside excellent writings by Kennan, Zuckerman and Emma Rothschild, there has been a good deal of patient rehearsal of deterrence theory, but always in a liberal, restrained, sensitive sort of way.

What there has never been (unless I have overlooked it) is any direct presentation or analysis of the political alternatives proposed by the European peace movement. These have simply been closed out, by brusque gestures of rejection. For example, Theodore Draper ('Nuclear Temptations', January 19, 1984) refers to me as 'the swami of the British antinuclear movement', and goes on:

> Thompson has a wildly inaccurate version of the origin of 'deterrence theory'; he seems to think that the theory came about *after* 'Poseidon and Polaris, the SS-20, the cruise missiles, the neutron bomb' in order 'to excuse all these things'.

The reference is to my essay on 'Deterrence and Addiction' which appears on page 5 of my last collection, and perhaps Mr Draper found the passage so offensive that he could not read further?

I was arguing in this essay two propositions. First, that deterrence theory 'is not an *operative* theory: that is, it does not direct any nation's behaviour. It appears always as a gloss, as an *ex post facto* apologia, as a theoretical legitimation of actions which are taken for quite different reasons'. First came the Bomb, the theory came after it. First came 'technology creep', and the refinement of deterrent theory followed. Of course, the origins of deterrence theory go back to those earliest days, notably in the work of Bernard Brodie. But Brodie's essay (in *The Absolute Weapon*, 1946) was not the occasion for strategy meetings in the Pentagon and the Kremlin. As I stated in the same place, and at page 4 (which Draper surely read?), 'it was only *after* the Soviet Union also developed thermo-nuclear weapons that the theory of deterrence came into vogue'.

I was arguing, secondly, that deterrence theory was addictive and that, in its worst-case analysis, had now come to exert an independent force as ideology—as an *accelerator* for the nuclear arms race:

> There has never been a stationary state of mutual deterrence; instead there has been a ceaseless pursuit for advantage within that state. The operative pressures have come both from the regions of politics and ideology, and from the inertial thrust of research and development within the military-industrial complexes of the opposed powers. Deterrence theory did not give us Poseidon and Polaris, the SS-20, the cruise missiles, the neutron bomb. These were given to us by the 'alchemists' in the research laboratories, the arms lobbyists, the alarmist leader-writers and populist politicians, and by the inter-service competition of the military elites. Deterrence theory came in afterwards to excuse all these things.

The general case that I was arguing has received a notable confirmation from Lord Zuckerman who, as scientific adviser to successive governments, was actually there at the time. He wrote ('Nuclear Fantasies', *NY Review of Books*, June 14, 1984):

> During the twenty years or so that I myself was professionally involved in these matters, weapons came first and rationalizations and policies followed. Soon after the NATO alliance was formed, free-falling atomic bombs were introduced into the Western armory. Their addition to what was already there was not demanded by some new strategic theory. They were brought in because they were the most powerful destructive agents that were then available. . . First came the weapons; then they had to be fitted into a presumed tactical doctrine, which in turn had to be fitted into an illusory strategy, usually elaborated by armchair warriors.

And he goes on to say, a little later:

> In 1945 no one spoke about 'deterrent strategy'. . . I doubt if anyone in Whitehall had heard of Bernard Brodie, any more than it has been my experience that British political leaders religiously read the outpourings of American armchair strategists. To those who took the decisions, the atomic, and later the hydrogen, bombs were simply immensely powerful weapons which, if they had the means, nations just had to have.

These matters may be arguable, but it can be seen that the analysis which I offered (an analysis which had been influenced by Lord Zuckerman's earlier writings) was not the 'wildly inaccurate' chanting of a 'swami' but a sequence confirmed by some evidence. Mr Theodore Draper does not, in fact, usually write so wildly and inaccurately—he has made telling criticisms of Pentagon policies, and within the definitions imposed by deterrence theory he is one of the doves. But his footnote dismissal is characteristic of a general stance among American liberals. They dare not take one step beyond the confines of deterrence theory and its premises of an everlasting state of nuclear threat between the blocs. Once outside that reassuring enclosure they would enter an unknown and terrifying world, peopled by 'swamis' and staring-eyed Greens and even ex-Communists, without well-funded and prestigious conferences, and where the women might make them sit in circles on the floor. Hence they do not enter debate but curtly refuse it ('disgraceful', 'wildly inaccurate'), putting up a set of concrete mind-blocks along the outer edge of deterrence theory to mark the limits between liberalism and the 'no go' regions. But in refusing debate, they refuse also to engage with any real world of politics, ideology, arms procurement. They must linger on the liberal margins of the deterrence enclosure, elaborating a discourse which is by turns techno-strategic (in which they will always be amateurs) and scholastic—an extraordinary abstracted speculation upon worst-cases, perceptions, bluffs and hypothetical intentions. They refuse to acknowledge that there could be alternatives, and, in doing so, they simply wall out the discourse of the European and American peace movements.

Mr George W. Ball, another 'moderate' of this kind, acclaimed Wieseltier's book as 'an impressive tour de force', and he especially commended the author for his 'disdain for E.P. Thompson who, like Schell, "argues backward from the apocalypse" to arrive at the "disgraceful" solution of unilateral disarmament' (*NY Review of Books*, February 2, 1984). Wieseltier follows the norm in drawing his readers' particular attention to my former membership of the Communist Party. But he is kind enough to hasten on and add: 'Thompson's ideological biography does not discredit his ideas; they discredit themselves.' And in support of this discreditable operation, he pokes around with a stick among my writings of the past decades and pulls out a few sentences from their contexts to put on display.

Most of these sentences are from my 'Open Letter to Leszek Kolakowski', of 1973. This 'Open Letter' is my most extended reflection upon Communism and anti-Communism, it has been republished in *The Poverty of Theory*, and readers who wish to put Wieseltier's samples into their context may consult it. I would change very little in it today, and a part of my argument (as to the potential for democratisation repressed within Communist forms) has been vindicated by the phenomenon of Solidarnosc.

What puzzled me when I read Wieseltier was a sense of familiarity—not only that I had written those selected lines ten years before, but that I had read them more recently. Turning back to *Commentary* I found that every one of Wieseltier's five selected sentences were among those selected by Mr Scott McConnell in his identical operation. This is too much to be put down to coincidence. Yet Wieseltier, in a full set of footnotes, makes no acknowledgement of his debt to McConnell, perhaps because the readers of the *New Republic* like to suppose themselves to be a little on the liberal side of *Commentary*?

What this suggests to me is that Wieseltier has not consulted with a candid mind my pre-1980 writings at all, unless to thumb through one essay and check the passages which McConnell had already marked. He is, like Heseltine and Frost, just flashing signals. And what are these terrible signals? In one of these selected snippets I am quoted as saying (of the Soviet Union), 'Fifty years is too short a time to judge a new social system.' What I had written was that there is 'one consideration'—

> Which is in a sense insulting to living and suffering people [which] is simply that, to a historian, fifty years is too short a time to judge a new social system, if such a system is arising. The comparison of

> course is with the protracted and contradictory events which signalled the arrival of capitalism-as-system onto the historical scene.

That is a philosophical consideration, which occupied half a paragraph in a 100-page essay, and which I readily agree offers no comfort to anyone living or dead. It does not take one far, and I did not follow it. But it is not an improper reflection to pass through a historian's head, nor to be placed on some Index of Impermissible Thoughts. It is made the occasion, by both authors, for paroxysms of polemic. Thus McConnell:

> Fifty years was ample time to consolidate the revolution, murder the socialist opposition, eliminate all freedoms of speech and publication, shut down the elected parliament, destroy the agricultural system, conquer and collectivize a dozen neighbouring countries, establish a gargantuan system of slave labour, commit political murders on a Hitlerian scale, and, finally, brandish a nuclear arsenal unprecedented in size at every nation in the world where people are free to elect their rulers.

And thus Wieseltier:

> Thompson is pretty serene. . . about the satanic statistics of Stalin's reign—fifty years may be too short a time to judge a new social system, but it was ample time to kill maybe a hundred million people. . .

If we leave aside the point that they are addressing a different question (I was asking whether, in the long historical perspective, the social system had a potential for evolution or self-transformation), these passages suggest authors for whom the display of self-righteous emotion is more important than reflection upon evidence. The USSR is not the only power which is brandishing an unprecedented nuclear arsenal, and Wieseltier's figures suggest that only a minority of the Soviet populace may ever be allowed to have died from natural causes. In a footnote he explains why he believes 'this almost unbelievable figure'. His total is totted up by including a figure of 32 millions who died in the Second

World War—a figure well in excess of generally-accepted estimates. It is an offence, not only against truth, but also against any possible reconciliation of minds with the Soviet people, for Western writers to suggest that these '32 million' victims of Hitler's invasion were killed by Communism's own malice.

Wieseltier also asserts that I believe that 'there is an equivalence of evil between the superpowers', and he dances around contrasting Communist totalitarian tyranny with American rights. It is curious that the same accusation provokes the fury of ideologists in the Communist world. According to the Czech Communist daily, *Rude Pravo* (August 25, 1984), I am a 'notorious anti-communist' working on behalf of 'the US Information Agency' (CIA) to 'influence the peace movement according to Washington's ideas':

> Thompson demands that the peace movement should be non-political and non-aligned and professes a theory of equal responsibility of the two 'superpowers'. Equal responsibility, equal distance, equal guilt—this is rhetoric which deliberately ignores the facts as to who unleashes new rounds of the arms race, although the facts strike one right in the eyes.

As it happens I have not ever argued about 'equal' responsibility, as if this were some nicely-calibrated 'balance' of moral missiles. I was willing to debate with Caspar Weinberger that 'there is no moral difference in the *foreign* policies' of the superpowers, although the words of that motion were chosen by the Oxford Union. There is no moral difference in foreign policies because both superpowers pursue, not morality, but their own interests. What we said, in the END Appeal (1980) was:

> We do not wish to apportion guilt between the political and military leaders of East and West. Guilt lies squarely upon both parties. Both parties have adopted menacing postures and have committed aggressive actions in different parts of the world.

Guilt lies squarely upon both parties, but that does not mean that guilt lies equally upon both at all times and for all things. Now one, now the other is more awful, and the Americans are generally gold medallists in the arms race Olympics while the Russians take the medals in the ideological marathon.

What I have argued is that the superpowers, and their attendant blocs, stand in a *reciprocal* relationship to each other, mutually inciting each others' armourers and ideologists, feeding upon each others' hostilities. In proposing this as a direction commanding whole societies, and as a logic of process, I may have abstracted the pressure of this logic from the full social context, and suggested a determinism which would render the efforts of the peace movement futile. I have sought to correct this in 'Exterminism Reviewed' (*The Heavy Dancers*,* p. 135). But I have never at any time suggested an identity or an 'equivalence of evil' (Wieseltier) in the opposing societies. How did we get into such an absurd non-question?

We got into it, I think, because Wieseltier's kind of anti-Communism requires that emotion expend itself in repeated public displays of moral abhorrence of the Other, and that this is its own sufficient end. Yet even if all that McConnell and Wieseltier say about the past fifty years of Soviet history is true (and some part of it is, give or take 32 million lives), what is left unsaid is that the Soviet Union has changed in extensive ways since Stalin's death, the *gulags* have shrunk, the 'disappeared ones' are now few, there are even some fragile rules and norms of law, and the cultural potential is changing all the time. This might be a moment, not for strengthening 'deterrence', but for strategies to moderate the political relations between the blocs.

But the very notion of this throws Wieseltier into a new moral apoplexy, provoked, on this occasion, not by myself but by Mr George Kennan. For Kennan has offended by arguing that 'we have to put an end to the often systematic

---

* My notions were exposed to criticism by many authors in the collection *Exterminism and Cold War* (Verso/NLB, 1982). The discussion has now been carried forward vigorously by Ken Coates, 'The Peace Movement and Socialism', in *The Most Dangerous Decade* (Spokesman, 1984).

condemnation of another great people and its government—a condemnation which if not stopped will really make war inevitable by making it seem inevitable'. But (says Wieseltier) to 'put an end to the systematic condemnation' of the Soviet Union 'is to put an end to the telling of the truth'. He accuses Kennan of pleading that, 'Because of the possibility of nuclear war, the United States may do nothing, in words or in deeds, to express its profound philosophical differences with the Soviet Union.' And if the United States were to follow Kennan's advice and 'exercise restraint in the tragic question of human rights', this would 'deprive the victims. . . of their only hope'.

The key to this passage may be found in the last three words, 'their only hope'. It has a self-congratulatory resonance. It massages the American ego to know that they are the 'only hope' of all those myriads without 'human rights'. As Mr Wieseltier crosses the campus, or perhaps walks back from his publisher, his breast must swell with pride to know that he is 'the only hope' of countless victims. But I do not know that he is. Nor even that America is. For many 'victims' in the Communist world, American cold war heroics are only a pain. They make their situation worse, by identifying them as suspect sympathisers with the Other. They offer no way, no way at all, of transforming the Communist world. With the exception of a few individuals, and the major and important exception of the Jewish emigration, these heroics have hindered the cause of 'human rights' more then they have helped. And the Jewish emigration from the Soviet Union, by draining out tens of thousands of gifted and internationally-minded people (who certainly had the right to live where they chose) did nothing to assist the renewal of Soviet society. The only society that it may have transformed is Brighton Beach in Brooklyn.

I do not wish American citizens to cease to be concerned with human rights. I only wish that the United States *government* would shut up. From our standpoint, neither President Reagan nor Mr Chernenko look like profound philosophers. Mr Kennan is, of course, right; the business of governments is to deal in a business-like way with their international interests and relations, and not to pronounce each other 'evil empires' or 'sworn enemies' in the advance of a declaration of war. If American and Soviet philosophers wish to argue about their profound differences, then let them do so directly as philosophers and not as the catspaws of states.

A great deal of humbug is stirred up when states become involved in philosophy, whether the universals of 'socialism' or 'human rights'. I strongly support commitment to human rights, when it comes from informed voluntary agencies, like Amnesty International or Helsinki Watch, or from the solidarity actions of citizens. But the NATO politicians who engage in a *jihad* against Communists on grounds of human rights are guilty of transparent hypocrisy, and on at least four counts. First, for their double-standards which are too notorious to merit discussion. (There are more political prisoners today in Turkey, NATO's loyal ally, than in any East European nation—and that is before we look into Latin America or Asia.) Second, these politicians celebrate movements in Communist countries, such as the huge self-management movements of Solidarnosc, which they would put down with riot police in their own. (As Mrs Thatcher's government has recently been demonstrating.) Third, NATO's professed ardour is a bluff which has long been called: Hungary (1956), Prague (1968), and so on. And any 'dissidents' with any sense know it. Fourth, NATO's cold warriors need the suffering of the victims and want it to go on. It is the strongest card in the whole cold war pack. It is good for war business and it is good for their own self-image. 'Human rights' are for NATO politicians the 'last refuge of the scoundrel'. They are good for the election of Presidents.

The 'only hope' of the victims does not rest in Mr Wieseltier nor in President Reagan but *in themselves*. If the Communist world is to be democratised or transformed, this will be done, in their own time and in their own way, by their own peoples. The help that can be brought from outside is small, and it will not be brought by a self-congratulatory Other with a Pershing II in his right hand and Central American blood on his left. The damage that can be brought from outside is immense. It is being brought by cold warriors every day. It is here that the Western peace movement has a different entitlement and might even be of some small service. By initiating an alternative healing-process it might loosen the bonds of security and open the windows of communication. Human rights are a proper concern of the peace movement, not as a precondition for disarmament but as *part of the process of making peace.*

This alternative way, which is neither the addiction to deterrence nor surrender, is one which Wieseltier's mind is simply incapable of receiving. Anti-Communism blocks entry to the ideas which many Europeans have been proposing, and he can only deal with us by beating up the favourite straw man of the century, 'Better Red than Dead'.

> Neutralism—or, as Thompson prefers, 'internationalism' [There is a difference. E.P.T.]—is presented as a logical requirement of disarmament. So, too, is 'better Red than dead'; or, as one of Thompson's lieutenants in European Nuclear Disarmament said, 'better Finnish than finished'. So, too, is the idea of unilateral disarmament. Unilateralism is a disgraceful notion, produced by people who think so little of themselves that they believe in nothing except life. Neutralism is an admission of philosophical exhaustion. Staying above the war of ideas is not a spiritual triumph; it is a spiritual collapse. It represents a loss of interest in the principles at stake in political systems. And 'better Red than dead' is an insult to those who believe 'better dead than Red'. . . It is not only a response to the threat of extinction; it is an attitude towards public life which affects the moral and psychological preparedness to resist totalitarianism at any time.

That is a mouthful, written by a very self-confident moralist. But whose ideas is he writing about? What is he writing against? There is one quotation, 'better Finnish than finished' which is attributed in his footnotes to 'Jolyan Howarth. . . in a conversation with the author'. When I confronted Dr Jolyon Howorth with this passage he was astonished, partly to find such a witticism (of which he had no recollection) attributed to him, but much more to discover that he was my 'lieutenant'. He could recall a heated conversation one night at Harvard with someone who did not listen and he supposed that this could have been Wieseltier.

There are three distinct issues in this package: neutralism, unilateralism and 'Better Red than Dead'. We will take them in inverse order. Since the Western peace movement is such a motley, diverse crowd it is probable that some persons somewhere have been saying 'Better Red than Dead'.* I have never seen it on a banner, or in the movement's literature, nor heard it from a platform. Wieseltier knows, or could know if he did any reading, that it is not an axiom supported by any responsible peace movement. He knows perfectly well that he will find nothing like it in my own writings, which is why he has recourse to the stratagem of attributing a quite different witticism, without permission, to an unrecorded private conversation with someone whom he describes, in absurd military terminology, as my 'lieutenant'. These are disreputable procedures.

I do not know who first invented the phrase. It was around in the late Fifties in Britain, when it was employed against CND by the peace movement's *opponents.*† And it has been employed in this way ever since. To those who are working for an alternative to both, it is of course a trick question, very much like 'Have you stopped beating your wife?', to which no answer is possible. It is also a question which confuses the individual choice with the general case. When in the late Fifties Professor A.J.P. Taylor, who was then active in CND, was asked it by a hostile interviewer, he is reported to have replied that he personally would opt

* Christa Wolf, in an entry dated April 1981, refers to 'Better Red than Dead' as a 'West German catch phrase you often hear these days': *Cassandra* (Virago, 1984).

† Bertrand Russell has sometimes been accused of originating the phrase. Ken Coates, of the Russell Peace Foundation, has pointed out to me, in a private communication, that Russell was at pains, on several occasions, to refute the suggestion. Thus he wrote in *Unarmed Victory* (1963, p. 50) of American attitudes of 'firmness' against Communism: 'They had been indoctrinated with the pernicious belief that only the American way of life can be tolerated. The only other point of view that they saw lay in the attitude "better red than dead"—a slogan which has been fathered upon me, although it is not mine but a translation of the slogan of a hostile German journalist. I believe in the possibility of co-existence.'

for death rather than surrender to a Communist occupation, but that neither he nor any government had the right to take this personal decision on behalf of a whole population, including the infants and the unborn.

It is an axiom, then, which lives as a taunt employed by polemicists *against* the peace movement, and the intention is to display us as defeatists or cowards and to close off any discussion of alternatives. There is also a trick of language here. In English the jaunty rhyme is clearly half-polemic, half-jest. But in French *(plutôt rouge que mort)* it has lost all taint of wit, and it can then be laid out with solemnity upon the shelves of *Paris Match* or *Art Press* as an example of the 'slogan' adopted by English (or American or German) *pacifistes*—a specimen to be dissected with elaborate philosophical disquisitions as to the subterfuges, liaisons and self-delusions of the human soul, and, in particular, as to the Anglo-Germanic threat to Parisian post-Maoist café culture. *Le pacifisme* is a disease against which France must be 'vaccinated', and M. André Glucksmann (who has suffered from most known ideological diseases in his time) is ready with the vaccine, culled from his own blood.

The present dissociation between French and other West European political cultures, and the misrecognitions between them, is indeed a problem, and one which must be overcome.* The Parisian intelligentsia has got into some complacent and provincial habits. In some directions it is deaf to any discourse which has not been approved by the priests of the local cults. In other directions it is sensitive, even to excess; it does indeed (if tardily) concern itself with human rights; it gave far more support to the Polish renewal (and its aftermath) than the British or German intelligentsia did; and it has remembered Afghanistan when others have forgotten. And for this reason the French language is a carrier of concepts (including *le pacifisme*) to some of our friends

---

* See the excellent discussions in Jolyon Howorth and Patricia Chilton (eds.), *Defence and Dissent in Contemporary France* (Croom Helm, 1984); Jolyon Howorth, *France: the Politics of Peace* (Merlin/END, 1984); and in Diana Johnstone, *The Politics of Euromissiles*, Chapter Three.

in East Europe, who naturally suppose that what the French tell them must be true and of good report.

There is a trick of language here also. *Le pacifisme*, *les pacifistes allemagnes*, confuse the concepts of pacifism and of the peace movement. I am told by another 'lieutenant' (that is, friend), Dr Paul Chilton, that *le pacifisme*,

> Appears to lump together the whole range of attitudes towards defence and security to be found in the peace movement and implies that they are all 'pacifist' in the strict sense that they reject all forms of defence through physical force. In contrast with most utilisations of the word *pacifism* in English, the French utilisation, however, has an invariably pejorative meaning. It is thus hard, for example, to predicate the word of oneself or one's group: to say 'je suis pacifiste' is as odd in many contexts as to say 'I am a treacherous coward'.

Because of the weight of a particular political and linguistic inheritance, *le pacifisme* can be employed pejoratively, to imply something a little more than 'surrender' and only a little less than 'quisling'. That is, the axiom 'better Red than Dead' appears to be already built in to it. And since the loudest peace movement in France, the *Mouvement de la paix*, is, unlike that in any other West European country, a Communist-dominated movement with a pro-Moscow inheritance, some of whose actors are certainly 'Red', this seems to confirm the linguistic shift. It is against all these problems that our friends in the non-aligned French movement, CODENE, must contend.

It is a tragic misrecognition that the complex political enterprise of the non-aligned peace movements should have been caricatured as 'Better Red than Dead'. This is perhaps because a vocal portion of the French intelligentsia has blindfolded its eyes with the words *le pacifisme* and has passed on this lazy libel to their friends in the East. But the same blindfold obscures the vision of the liberal apologists for 'deterrence theory' in the United States. These basic 'cold war assumptions' were long ago identified by Father Thomas Merton:

> The first and greatest of all commandments is that America shall not and must not be beaten in the Cold War, and the second is like

> unto this if a hot war is necessary to prevent defeat in the Cold War then a hot war must be fought even if civilization is to be destroyed. . . The one great 'reality' is the threat of Communism, and all else is illusion, fantasy, speculation, theory or what you will. . . It amounts almost to an obsession and this is what really worries me most: so many good and reasonable and intelligent and well trained minds are held captive by this absolute principle which makes them unable to. . . take any other viewpoint than that of cold war military practicality.*

It is because of this 'obsession' that intelligent minds block out the consideration of any possible alternative, and when they encounter certain key-words, such as 'unilateral', they react with knee-jerks: 'disgraceful!' This is strange, since for thirty-odd years the multiplication of nuclear weaponry has been going on by unilateral additions on one side or the other. Among the intelligent minds which have recently contributed to nuclear debate are those of Mr Robert MacNamara and Mr George W. Ball. Both of course are convicted unilateralists, since they were in office—Mr MacNamara as Secretary for Defense and Mr Ball as US Under Secretary of State—during a period of unprecedented US nuclear armament, carried through unilaterally and justified by falsified estimates as to a 'missile gap'. It has been estimated that in the period 1960–1964 United States ICBMs increased from 18 to 834 (the Soviet Union's complement increasing, also unilaterally, from 4 to 200), while US tactical nuclear warheads in Europe increased from 2,500 to 7,000.† I do not point this out in order to disallow MacNamara and Ball's voices in the current debate (I find Mr MacNamara's recent confessions and second thoughts to be moving and honourable). But I do so in order to plead with them to show more humility towards those of us who, in those same years, were arguing that unilateral refusals or subtractions, rather than additions, might further the cause of peace.

---

* Thomas Merton to W.H. Ferry, March 6, 1962, in *Letters from Tom*, ed. W.H. Ferry (Scarsdale, 1984).

† A cogent summary of this period is in Robert Neild, *How to Make Up Your Mind about the Bomb* (1981), pp. 23–27.

Mr Ball, however, follows Mr Wieseltier in finding 'the idea of unilateral disarmament. . . a disgraceful notion'. And this is taken, unexamined. I cannot rebuke American commentators for supposing that the policy of the West European peace movement, and in particular of British CND as well as the British Labour Party, is that of 'unilateral disarmament', since this has frequently been reported as uncontested fact, not only by the American media, but also, to the British public (in particular during the General Election of 1983) by such agencies as the publicly-financed British Broadcasting Corporation (which has a pretence of being non-partisan).

But the policy of CND and of the British Labour Party is *not* 'unilateral disarmament'. It may help to clarify this point if I reproduce some passages of an article which I published in the *Observer* in November 1983 in response to a column by Mr Conor Cruise O'Brien.

> CND's most famous doctrinal commitment ('unilateral nuclear disarmament') is a recommendation to *this* nation [i.e. Britain]. Like most doctrines it should be understood in its historical origin. It was the founding charter of CND, over 25 years ago, and was graven on tablets by Bertrand Russell, Canon Collins, A.J.P. Taylor, J.B. Priestley, Peggy Duff, James Cameron and the other founders.'
>
> It was, in origin, the first demand to stop 'proliferation'. America and Russia had "the Bomb" (and it is interesting to recall that It used to be thought of in the singular). If Britain were to set an example by refusing the Bomb, then this might seal off further proliferation.* It is tragic for us—and perhaps for the world—that CND, first time around, did not win.
>
> CND remains loyal to its founders' charter. It continues to argue, cogently, that nuclear weapons are a suicidal property upon this island; are obscene; and that a non-nuclear defence would greatly enhance our national security.
>
> This policy is not 'unilateral disarmament' (as TV presenters snicker) but unilateral *nuclear* disarmament; and this, not for one

* The ineffable Mr Gerald Frost, who is still maundering on in *Encounter*, and who cannot write three words without getting one wrong, offers to correct an earlier folly (*Encounter*, 'Letters', Sept–Oct 1984) by saying: 'As for "all those marches to Aldermaston", most of them were not *to* the Aldermaston US Air Force base, but *from*. . .'. They were of course from the (British) Aldermaston Weapons Research Establishment, and they were in protest against the manufacture of British nuclear weapons.

> bloc in the Cold War confrontation only (without reciprocation from the other bloc) but for *this* country—as an initiative to get the multilateral thing moving.
>
> That ought to be clear, although the media make it as clear as mud.
>
> It is also of interest that CND's policy is more radical, on this point, than many other sections of the Western peace movement. Few major European movements are 'unilateralist'—partly because they don't inhabit nuclear-weapons-owning nations. The majority Italian and Belgian movements agitate for 'balanced reductions'. The Dutch movement has a policy similar to CND ('let's get rid of nuclear weapons from the world, starting with Holland!') but the German movement is, essentially, united around the demand to stop Pershing II and cruise, while the United States majority movement works for a freeze.

That still seems to me to put the position plainly. Some imperfectly-informed observers suppose that 'the peace movement' has one single, abstract, universal platform (which is then sometimes described as 'unilateral*ism*', as if a tactic or national strategy could be presented as a philosophical '*ism*'!). But all that is universal in this multitude of movements, with their differing national accentuations, is the world-wide growth of peace consciousness, with its dimensions of fear, love and hope and its refusal of the means of genocide.

This globe is not going to get rid of nuclear weapons in one single move, like cutting a tape with scissors. It is entirely proper that different national movements will adopt differing policies: thus, Scandinavian and Balkan movements are concerned with regional nuclear-free zones; the Spanish movement is interested in moving Spain out of NATO to add her influence to the non-aligned nations such as Sweden, Yugoslavia and Austria; some of our friends in the East are more concerned with ideological disarmament (with 'dialogue' and the building of 'trust'); while the movements in West Germany are preoccupied with various proposals for healing the wound of Central Europe (demilitarised corridors? a new Rapacki-style zone? the neutralisation of both Germanies?). The largest British movement, CND, has long supported the refusal of all nuclear weapons on British soil and waters.

The reasons for CND's policy (which is now endorsed by the British Labour Party and by several smaller political parties) have been written out with patience and by many expert hands. British 'independent' nuclear weapons (which are not independent) are a nostalgic and expensive imperial status symbol, while American weapons on our territory subvert our independence and reduce us to cliency. Since there is now a grotesque surplus of weaponry in Europe this affords space for certain nations (Britain and Holland) to get rid of them, without endangering any notional 'balance' between the superpowers, in the hope of initiating an alternative (and reciprocal) process of multilateral disarmament. For decades the superpowers have ignored all other nations (even their dearest allies) and bored the world to death with 'negotiations' whose only outcome has been to legitimate the absurd increment of weapons. We envisage unilateral refusals (that is, unilateral subtractions instead of additions) as a means of negotiating directly by *actions*, and in the hope of calling forth some response.

CND's policy of unilateral refusal is a policy for Britain, and we have not set up an export agency to impose our policy on peace workers in other nations. It is true that from time to time we have recommended to both superpowers immediate unilateral initiatives (negotiation by actions) as a means of getting the reciprocal process going. Some of us approve of Charles Osgood's GRIT strategy (graduated reductions in tension) by which one power or another makes a substantial unilateral reduction in some weapons-system, holds the ratchet, and awaits a response. (There is abundant fat in every system to try these things.) If the majority of American peace workers consider that the freeze is the most viable strategy, then that is their affair and we will not interfere. So long as they understand that this is *their* strategy, and it does not therefore have to be *ours*. If the superpowers could only agree to STOP, and to hold the arms equilibrium steady, this might be precisely the time when intermediate lesser powers can run down their stocks and make a space of quiet between the giants.

It will be seen that what harmonises in this ill-conducted orchestra of European (and, increasingly, Asian, Australasian and Third World) movements is the mounting pressure to move out from under, and to resume some national autonomy. For decades the superpowers have glared at each other, eyeball to eyeball, over our heads. It now seems to be beyond the mental capacity of some Americans and some Russians to allow entry to the notion that there might be some other ball-game than their own. This mental prohibition affects the hawks and doves of both Establishments alike. The hawks shift their client states around, and deposit their nuclear stool on their territories (Britain, Sicily, both Germanies, Czechoslovakia) at will. The doves elaborate 'arms control' agendas, in which the clients remain unconsulted but controlled. They do not mind a little non-alignment, if it seems to tip the balance of things their own way: Romania is applauded by NATO for making faces at SS-20s, Greece is applauded by Soviet leaders for making faces at American bases. But authentic independent initiatives which call in question the whole ball-game draw down the anathemas of both houses.

I find that these anathemas are visited, with increasing frequency, upon my own white head. Week after week they plop through the letter-box, some from one side, some from the other. It is unnerving to find that I am a target for the ideological missiles of both blocs. When I am working in my Worcestershire garden and a helicopter hovers overhead, I am tempted to run and hide. It might be theirs or it might be theirs, but it cannot be one of ours because all we have are typewriters and marching feet.

The Soviet ideologists do not trouble with the niceties of argument but go straight into political hard-porn. Mr Yuri Zhukov, the President of the Soviet Peace Committee has recently explained in *International Life* (June 1984) that 'having made a painful reappraisal of the current situation, U.S. and NATO psychological warfare units are attempting to sabotage some of the anti-nuclear movements from the inside, smuggling their own instructions and ideas into them'. I am singled out for attention by Mr Zhukov as a leader of one of these 'units', and Mr G. Lokshin, the Secretary of this same peace-loving Committee, adds the names of the Bertrand Russell Peace Foundation; the British END Committee; Mr Mient-Jan Faber, the general secretary of the Dutch Interchurch Peace Council (IKV); and, for good measure, the IPCC (International Peace Communications and Coordination Centre), an office in The Hague which brings into regular conferences nearly all the major European (as well as some American) non-aligned peace movements, including the Norwegian, Swedish, Danish, Italian, Spanish, West German, Belgian, Swiss, Finnish, Irish, French CODENE and British CND. (I am sorry about all these acronyms, but the European peace movement is now a complex beast.) I am simply pointing out that Mr Zhukov and Mr Lokshin have just 'unmasked' a quite extraordinary conspiracy in which the most powerful European peace movements turn out to be under the control of 'US and NATO psychological warfare units'.

Mr Lokshin's article gives more details as to how this has come about:

> In NATO's arsenal of methods of subversion directed against the anti-war movement, an ever-greater place is being given to ideological warfare. This is carried out partly with the help of various front organizations and groups that insinuate themselves into the anti-war movement. . . E.P. Thompson, an English historian and sociologist, widely publicized of late, a former professor at Oxford University [not guilty. E.P.T.], is the noisiest mouthpiece of these anti-Soviet conceptions. As to the views of this Thompson concerning the internal political situation in the USSR—views which he strenuously advertises on any convenient occasion—these are simply a mixture of absolute ignorance with the basest of lies spread by Cold War professionals. (*International Life*, June 1984).

I do not mind so much about this invective, which is the only language Soviet ideologists know how to employ. I have got used to it over the years. As long ago as 1958 a writer in *Novy Mir* unmasked me as a 'renegade', 'traitor', 'anarchist' and 'philosophising slanderer', and the file has been kept up-to-date ever since. But I will admit that I do somewhat resent the suggestion that I, and END, and the

Russell Foundation are 'agents of NATO and imperialism... infiltrated by Western Secret Services' into a movement which, in its present form, we helped to start.

As for myself, I was 'infiltrated' into the peace movement in 1945, when Britain intervened in the civil war in Greece, and have been there, in one capacity or another, through the times of Korea and German re-armament, the first wave of CND, and the Vietnam War. As I look back down those forty years I could even be bitter that wars and the threat of nuclear war have eaten half of the lives of myself, my family and my closest friends.

But I mean to go on. I am willing even—distasteful as it would be—to talk once again with Mr Zhukov and Mr Lokshin, if an occasion should arise when it might be productive of any good. This occasion may well not arise, since (Mr Lokshin explains to his Soviet readers) Mient-Jan Faber and I are currently preoccupying ourselves with attempts to pull the anti-war movement—

> into an authentic 'crusade' against the socialist fraternity, while cynically hiding themselves behind stolen banners of peace. E. Thompson incites his listeners by saying: 'We have to begin acting as if a unified, neutral and peaceful Europe already existed'.

So that we now know the full measure of my anti-Soviet incitements. As it happens this terrible phrase is not strictly mine (although I first drafted it) but is taken from the European Nuclear Disarmament Appeal of April 1980:

> We must commence to act as if a united, neutral and pacific Europe already exists. We must learn to be loyal, not to 'East' or 'West', but to each other, and we must disregard the prohibitions and limitations imposed by any national state.

I have already noted that this Appeal was signed by thousands across the continent (and also in Australia, Japan and the USA) and so far from being 'infiltrated' at a late stage was a major initiative setting the movement in motion.

This Appeal signalled that the signatories—and the movements which ensued—were no longer content to play on either side of the superpower ball-game. Nor were we even content to watch from the sidelines and say 'shush' to both parties. We were setting up a new game in a different place, in which we were going to attempt to make peace between citizens in contempt of the blocs and their ideologies; and we explicitly declared that 'we must defend and extend the right of all citizens, East or West, to take part in this common movement and to engage in every kind of exchange'. As for the political stance of a peaceful Europe, I would today prefer the term 'non-aligned' to 'neutral', since it signifies an active, peace-making diplomacy, a third way, rather than a passive opting-out in the hope of self-preservation.

It is here that we must return (I must hope for the last time) to the Little Blue Book of Chairman Wieseltier. For Wieseltier is quite as scandalised by me as are Comrades Zhukov and Lokshin. He indicts me as an advocate of European 'neutralism', which he takes to mean that 'there is no need to take sides in the struggle between the United States and the Soviet Union if it makes no difference who wins'. This is a remarkably silly statement. If there is a 'struggle' between the US and the USSR, which must be fought out to some 'winning' finish, then this is a disaster for both parties; and if either side were to 'win' it would be a total disaster for Europe, culturally, spiritually, materially, and politically. It is a no-win situation. Europeans are bored by this Pretend War, and are increasingly alarmed by it (since it might at any moment become real). They wish neither the USA nor the USSR to 'win' it, and they are forming some notion of mediating between these overmighty strugglers and of asking them both to go home.

But 'neutralism', for Wieseltier, 'is an admission of philosophical exhaustion. Staying above the war of ideas is not a spiritual triumph; it is a spiritual collapse. It represents a loss of interest in the principles at stake in political systems'. No, Mr Wieseltier: you are a specimen case of the 'obsession' against which Father Thomas Merton has warned us. You project your American ego upon the world, just as Zhukov projects the ego of Soviet man, and presume to impose upon it a 'struggle' in which there may be only two 'sides': the Other and your own. You have the presumption to impose this same stunted binary definition of 'the principles at stake in political systems' upon the intellectual and spiritual world: once again, there can be only two 'sides', the Other and your own, and 'the war of ideas' must be a war between only such ideas as will pass muster with the sidesmen. Has it never occurred to you, Mr Wieseltier, that there might be three sides, or four, or five? Is there some binary determinism in the human mind which breeds this Soviet-American arrogance? How did the great globe, in all its historical diversity, shrivel (in the minds of Soviet and American ideologists) into the two halves of a Manichean walnut?

It is perhaps true that there is a certain 'loss of interest in the principles at stake in political systems', if the only systems admitted to view are those of the United States and the Soviet Union. This 'loss of interest' may be felt, not only in Europe, but throughout the world, and not least among the publics of these nations. Yet it is arrogant in Wieseltier to conclude that this signals 'a spiritual collapse' among the lesser breeds without the law. What makes for anxiety is the sense that we are witnessing, in very different ways, the spiritual collapse of *both* systems under the weight of their obsessional confrontation—a collapse which will drag us all down together.

The obsession which may destroy the world is precisely this: that there may be only two 'sides'. This is to enforce a closure upon all alternative lines of political and spiritual growth, and to lock the blocs onto an inexorable collision-course. American and Soviet ideologists, who ceaselessly strive to conscript all human resources to one side or the other, are genuinely unaware that in doing so they may be writing the death-warrant of their own civilizations. For their own future, as well as that of Europe and the Third World, may depend upon new forces and new spaces entering in between the adversaries, pressing them gently apart, and enabling them to unlock from their death-wishing struggling.

That is what we suppose that we are attempting, in the European peace movements. As the ideological missiles of both sides plop through our postboxes it scarcely seems that we are 'staying above the war of ideas'. We appear to have touched that war at such a sensitive place that both Mr Zhukov and Mr Wieseltier forget to 'struggle' with each other and combine their forces to struggle against us.

Both of these mighty strugglers reveal the imperial mentality of the superpowers. Mr Zhukov considers that the European peace movements ought to be auxiliaries of Soviet diplomacy and, indeed, pay deference to his leadership. He is scandalised, and the entire official Communist and World Peace Council apparatus is scandalised, by the suggestion that there could be co-responsibility by both superpowers for the world's predicament. Mr Wieseltier is no less scandalised. He announces, as a theorem which admits of no discussion, that 'for moral ends the United States has made an extraordinary commitment to Europe'. This 'commitment' is witnessed by the nuclear excreta which the United States had deposited on the lands and seas of Western Europe. These represent a commitment to 'extended' deterrence, which locks West Europe and America together in the war of Two Camps.

And so indeed it does. I will not follow Mr Wieseltier into his chapter on 'The Case of Europe', since it is spectacularly ill-informed. Several of his assertions are so misleading that they rival certain press conferences of President Reagan (in which he asserted that on 'their' side there were umpteen hundred SS-20s and on 'our' side there was—nothing!), and it is difficult to see how anyone pretending to intellectual credentials could descend lower than that.* What I wish to note, once again, is Wieseltier's self-congratulatory tone.

* Wieseltier says (of 1983) that 'the intermediate-range missiles of the Russians are met only by the long-range missiles of the Americans' bringing Western Europe into 'a single-hostage relationship' to the Soviet Union. He pretends not to have heard of Poseidon nor of several air and sea-based systems nor of the British and French systems, nor of the multitude of 'tactical' systems. He could have enlightened himself by consulting several of the works cited in his own notes, including my own *Protest and Survive.*

He is becoming 'bitter' with all Europeans: with the peace movements because they show ingratitude to the 'moral ends' of the U.S. of A., and with West European governments because they will not jump to the orders of General Bernard Rogers and engage in a massive build-up of their conventional forces. West Europe has to have cruise and Pershing 'because Europe is not prepared to take responsibility for its fate on its own'; Europeans 'prefer the nuclear peril to higher taxes'. They are willing to 'sacrifice' America 'for the sake of their standard of living'.

This is a difficult argument because there are at least three parties to it and not two: the United States, West European governments, and the peace movements both in America and Europe. These parties do not share the same interests nor the same 'moral ends'. Mr Wieseltier is right to insist that the pro-Atlanticist governments of West Europe (and notably those of Chancellors Schmidt and Kohl, Mrs Thatcher and Mr Craxi) have been accomplices before, during, and after the act of NATO 'modernisation'. It does not follow that their interests are identical. As Lord Zuckerman has noted, those who are 'immediately informed about political and strategic issues' need not necessarily share 'what seems to be the official American view of the danger of the threat that the USSR poses to their security'. For the official American view appears to come out of the heads of arms promoters, populist politicians and intrepid ideologists but not from the heads of informed observers. Living closer to the Soviet Union than Washington does, and with more opportunities to observe the symptoms of Soviet weakness and the cruel mess which is developing in Eastern Europe, common sense as well as respect for their taxes may suggest to European governments that this is not the moment to engage in a huge and provocative build-up of conventional armaments.

It is an odd situation when those who are most strident about the threat of the Other are the ideologues and politicians most remote from each other, not only in miles but in culture; whereas those supposed 'enemies' who are immediate neighbours have learned to sleep easily at night. It suggests that the Threat is continually reproduced and amplified within American and Soviet ideology. That is not to say that there is *no* threat, but that the threat is one which increments of missiles and ideological incitements only feed and make worse. As for the third party to this argument, the peace movement, Zuckerman is surely right to say that 'while most of the protesters are not sympathetic to communism they also do not give a hoot about the *jihad* against communism President Reagan has proclaimed. What worries them is the picture of trigger-happy Americans'. And they are also working on their *own* 'moral ends'.

Mr Wieseltier is a confident moralist. He is very confident about America's moral ends, and the radiance of this morality is reflected in his own self-approbation. I do not wish to undermine his moral ego. I am sure that he is a true believer in the principles of the Free World, and, for all that I know, his fellow-moralist, Mr Yuri Zhukov, is a true believer in the moral ends of Soviet Socialism.

I wish only to note the signs of an imperial mentality. It is one thing for a nation to cherish moral ends; it is another to seek to export them. To become insensitive to the moral ends of other nations, to hector them when they will not comply, to seek to impose upon other peoples one's own moral ends—this is immorality.

I cannot, as an Englishman and a historian, get into a lather about this. British imperial history is littered with moral ends. In Victorian and Edwardian times every British interest was vested in moralistic rhetoric as to our civilizing mission, every Gatling gun in the Transvaal and every British-held fleapit East of Suez was a 'moral end'. Nor was it all self-interested rhetoric: many of the moral missionaries were true believers, and a few of them dealt out honest coin. There was even, perhaps, a little 'civilizing' done. Both the imperial rulers and most of their domestic critics (the Liberals, Radicals and Fabians—I had almost added Democrats) shared in the same infection. The rulers taught the lesser breeds to obey and the reformers taught them how (in civilized and constitutional ways) they might press for reform. What was wrong was that it was our own 'moral ends' and not the ends opted for by other peoples which were consulted. Since we possessed the power, we imposed our own definition of legitimate ends upon others.

It is inevitable that American and Soviet rulers, and their missionary apologists, should fall victim to the same imperial mentality. Commanding unprecedented military power, reaching far into every part of the globe, United States rulers assume that the globe should be brought into compliance with their own ends. It is not a matter about which the British should show surprise. But the precedent should be borne in mind. It is the easiest thing in the world to dress up self-interest as a moral end. The Kissinger Commission's report on Central America lists as the first goal of United States policy in that tormented zone:

> To preserve the moral authority of the United States.
> To be perceived by others as a nation that does what is right *because* it is right is one of this country's principal assets.

However 'others' may perceive the United States, this self-perception is certainly a source of national self-approbation. It was one of the loudest themes of President Reagan's loud election: 'America will never give up its great mission, never.' And, invoking America's 'manifest destiny', he offered himself as Vice-Regent of 'the God who made us and who has blessed us as no other people on earth'. A few months before, Mr Caspar Weinberger conceded that 'there is no corner of the world so remote, no nation so insignificant, that it does not represent a vital interest of the United States'. The claim is one which would have brought a blush to the cheek of Cecil Rhodes. It is a chilling claim, when made by the War Minister of the most powerful nation ever known, fully capable of incinerating the earth.

Yet how is it possible that Mr Weinberger can assume this licence to intervene anywhere, by America's manifest right, unless he is, like his President, stupified beyond recall by the axiom that whatever America may do it must be for the 'moral end'? He is, like Mr Wieseltier, punch-drunk with imperial hubris, to the point that he does not know that the rest of the world is watching him in an odd way. And the world is right to be watchful. Imperial arrogance of this order is more vicious and more dangerous than racism, sexism and all other isms which honourable Americans so consciously resist, since it compounds them all.

It was in 1965 that Father Thomas Merton warned that 'the American illusion of innocence and universal messianism is now about to unleash THE worst war that ever happened, maybe the final one'. Thomas Merton got the timing wrong but the bearings right, and American messianism is still on course. Towards 'USS Messiah' there steams, on opposing course, the imperial supertanker of Soviet socialist teleology. At present in Europe we are contemplating the 'moral ends' jettisoned in the wake of these two generous superpowers. In the churned-up waters the cruise and Pershing missiles are now copulating with the SS-21s and SS-23s, and breeding on each others' vile bodies the next generations of missiles which will burn our children. There will follow, blessed by the moralists of both sides, the moral end of the world.

III 'ACTING AS FREE PERSONS'

The Soviet ideologues are quite as zealous only-two-sidesmen as are the most zealous apologists of NATO. They will not delay us long in argument, because argument is not their chosen medium. Confronted by the least suggestion of a third way, or of a third or fourth side, they resort instantly to slander or to political hard-porn ('CIA agents', 'NATO psychological warfare agencies', etc.). The most subtle variant of which they are capable is that of suggesting that well-meaning persons have been misled into positions which 'objectively serve the interests of. . .' (NATO, President Reagan, etc.) and which have 'nothing in common with' the positions of true 'peace champions'.

Thus Mr Lokshin, the Secretary of the Soviet Peace Committee, lamented the fact that some people were confused at CND's Annual Conference in Sheffield (December 1983) and others (identified with END) argued against the logic of 'balance' and 'persistently tried to convince us that the retaliatory measures of the Soviet Union [i.e. SS-21s and 23s on GDR and Czechoslovak territory] were allegedly unwarranted and even harmful':

> In the conditions of the unbridled anti-Soviet campaign conducted by the powerful propaganda machine of NATO countries, with the extremely limited possibilities to get truthful and objective information, the ranks of the peace champions are infiltrated with false ideas of the 'equal responsibility' of the USSR and USA. . . This is greatly influenced by all sorts of 'experts' who disguised under the

mask of 'objectivity' skilfully confuse not very experienced and misinformed people. . .

Of course, such pseudo-theoretical exercises, which fill pages of the publications issued for the anti-war activists, and which, under the guise of objectivity and so-called non-alignment, repeat the elements of NATO's official propaganda, inflict great damage on many sincere opponents of the arms race by confusing and disorienting them.

(*Twentieth Century and Peace*—the Organ of the Soviet Peace Committee—2/1984).

It is extraordinary—and a sign of its obsolescence—that Soviet ideological polemic has reduced the rich Russian language to these predictable and stagnant routines. It would be easy to say that it represents the mental reflexes of persons habituated to operating within a culture where arguments are settled by police measures or slander, rather than intellectual means; and if the vocabulary of 'masks' and 'disguises' and 'infiltration' is an indication of their own techniques of operation (perhaps within the Western peace movements?) then one must draw the most pessimistic conclusions.

Yet the curious thing is that the further one gets from public situations and official noises, the more flexible discussion may become. It is even possible to flush out from among the diplomats and officials of the 'peace' apparatus the occasional dove who (off-the-record, of course) allows a little reality to break in.

Hence this polemic is a language of public policy and of propaganda. It is not internalised. It is not a language of belief. It is a business pursued with failing conviction. The polemicists of 'peace' do not pretend to credibility, but they continue with their weary slanders because they fear that they could not control the consequences if an honest dialogue were to be thrown open between East and West. The tone of their exchanges becomes increasingly bitter, but also more brittle.

It may help readers if I outline, not so much the course of this polemic, as the events which occasioned it—the quarrelsome dialectic between alternative notions of the peace movement.

I have already described some of the ways in which the West European movement built itself up from non-aligned bases in 1980-1. Among the first few hundreds of international signatories to the European Nuclear Disarmament Appeal (April 1980) there was one solitary Soviet name: that of the courageous, independent-minded historian, Roy Medvedev. (His brother, Dr Zhores Medvedev, an involuntary exile in London, spoke at the Appeal's launching conference.) To borrow the language of our opponents, 'it is no accident that' this was the case. For an Appeal which laid guilt upon both parties, which not only called for the cancellation of NATO 'modernisation' (cruise and Pershing II) but also called on the Soviet Union to halt production of the SS-20 at its then total (of some 140 missiles), and which proclaimed that 'we must defend and extend the right of all citizens, East or West, to take part in this common movement and to engage in every kind of exchange', was unlikely to win the approval of the Soviet 'peace' apparatus.

But, as I have already noted, there has been some pro-Moscow influence in the Western peace movement, and it has been damaging and time-wasting. Some of this has come from the World Peace Council which, ever since early 1980, has been panting after the non-aligned movement, 'trying to catch hold of its coat-tails and to claim it as its own'. This Council was founded in the last years of Stalin, and has sought to impose its hegemony upon all peace movements ever since; it has offices in Helsinki, carbon-copy 'peace' committees in Communist countries, some influential affiliates in the Third World, two or three affiliates of influence in the West (including the French *Mouvement de la paix*) and a number of small unrepresentative committees without real grass-roots support (such as the British Peace Assembly and the American Peace Council).

The World Peace Council has been an organ of Soviet diplomacy for thirty years and there has never been any serious attempt to pretend that it is not. Indeed, this stance is justified on the grounds that the Soviet government's policies and proposals are in every respect the most peace-loving possible, and therefore the peace-loving masses of the world should rally to these. Neither the Council nor its Warsaw bloc affiliates have ever criticised in public any military measure or procurement on their own side, with the instructive exception of the Czechoslovak Peace Committee in 1968 which was at once disbanded. According to the tactics of the moment, the WPC may arrange international conferences which are more or less flexible in their appeal to 'all men and women of goodwill'. (The conferences promoted in Sofia, 1980, and Prague, 1983, may be examples.) But it has always been utterly inflexible in seeking to slander, contain or destroy any international peace initiative which offered alternative non-aligned perspectives.

A few authentically independent movements in the West have always sought to remain on good-neighbourly talking terms with the WPC, on the grounds that if the world is divided into two halves, someone must seek to keep open bridges of communication, however frail. These have included the International Fellowship of Reconciliation; the West German ASZ (Aktion Sühnezeichen); Western Christians co-operating with the Prague-based CPC (Christian Peace Conference). and of course the Quakers, notably the American Friends Service Committee and the British Quaker Peace and Service. (Lord Noel-Baker and Lord Brockway's World Disarmament Campaign entered into similar relations.) I make no objection to attempts at bridge-building if they are done with clear eyes and dignity, in the old Quaker spirit of 'speaking truth to power'. But sentimental efforts at East–West brokerage can be manipulated in damaging ways.

My favourite Quaker is the sturdy one who, when on shipboard in the early 19th century, found that his vessel was being boarded by pirates. Since his faith forbade him to take up arms he witnessed the scene with mounting impatience. At length, when one ruffian with a cutlass in his teeth swarmed over the side directly in front of him, he held out his hands with the quiet remark: 'Friend, thee hath no business here,' and pressed him gently back into the sea. I sometimes wish that today's Quakers would show the same courtesy to the World Peace Council ruffians who swarm up the sides of the good ship 'Peace'.

The unexpected emergence in 1980–1 of a Western peace movement from independent bases and with growing mass support was viewed by the East bloc establishment with perplexity. On the one hand, a surge of public opinion which was chiefly directed against NATO modernisation was clearly a bonus, and its supporters were not to be snubbed; on the other hand, the establishment viewed with acute suspicion a movement whose proponents included individuals and organisations committed to human rights (such as the Russell Peace Foundation and the West German 'Greens'), which made demands on Soviet militarism also, which sought to reach citizen opinion in the East, and whose members, at their demonstrations, wore the badge of Solidarnosc alongside the badges of peace. Attempts to bring the movement under World Peace Council leadership proved futile—almost no-one (except Bukovsky) was interested in that WPC event in Sofia—and open opposition would have been inopportune. The supporters of the WPC settled down to more quiet attempts to influence or manipulate the Western movement from within.

In this they met with a novel difficulty. Before 1968 it was usually possible to gain a major influence in Western peace movements by the dedication of committed Communist cadres in organising roles. But since the repression of the Prague Spring there has been a growth in Eurocommunism, one of whose leading principles has been the resistance to such kinds of Soviet manipulation. Hence the Eastern bloc establishment found that their attempts at influence were often resisted, not only by Greens and social-democrats and liberals, but also by Communists. In particular, the powerful Italian Communist Party threw its weight on the side of the non-aligned movement, as did many Eurocommunists in Spain, Finland, Britain and other countries. In certain countries the picture remained confused (for example, in West Germany where the pro-Soviet DKP long had an influence in the movement greater than its actual strength), whereas in Portugal and France, where pro-Moscow parties attempted an old-fashioned 'peace' operation, the result was to weaken the peace movement itself.

I will not waste time on the skirmishes of 1980–1. During that time the Soviet Union was steadily putting down more SS-20s, month by month. The litmus test between peace movements and 'peace' movements came to be between those which called publicly and in earnest for the halting or dismantling of SS-20s and those which forgot to mention them. Those of us who mentioned SS-20s, rather sharply, began to receive missives from the Soviet Peace Committee's office in Moscow, in language addressed to deaf children, patiently explaining that SS-20s were wholly defensive weapons developed 'in response to actions of the imperialist circles which aspire for world domination'.

On Hiroshima Day, 1981, the Dutch IKV and British END Committee issued an Appeal to all parties to cancel NATO modernisation and (to the Soviet government) to halt and commence reductions in SS-20s. We drew this Appeal to the attention of the Soviet Peace Committee and courteously invited their support: 'It is a frequent argument of our opponents. . . that peace organisations in the Soviet Union and in Eastern Europe direct their propaganda *only* against the military measures in the West and do nothing to make the same demands upon governments in the Warsaw alliance.' After a long silence END received a heavy response from Mr Oleg Kharkhardin, Vice-President of the SPC (December 11, 1981):

> Unlike anti-war public movements in the West, the Soviet peace movement exists in a country which has made the struggle for peace the basis of its foreign policy. . . No Soviet government would be able to conduct any policy other than one aimed at the security of our country and the strengthening of universal peace.

As for our Appeal in the matter of SS-20s, 'the Soviet people and their government will not agree to unilateral disarmament'.

Looking back, it is now possible to see October and November 1981 as the highest tide (until now) of the West European peace movement. Demonstrations took on epidemic proportions. There was a significant shift, an opening towards reconciliation with the East, in middle opinion. Polish Solidarity was still overground, giving rise to a hazy euphoria in which it seemed that Eastern societies were on the verge of great transitions. The defeat of NATO modernisation (then still two years ahead) seemed a practical political possibility—indeed, President Reagan sought to contain, not the SS-20s but the peace movement, with his 'zero option' in late November. A thaw in the cold war seemed to be almost within reach.

Euphoria ended on December 13th, 1981, with the hammer blow of martial law in Poland. A few months later Britain disappeared into the black hole of the Falklands War. By contrast with 1981, 1982 was a bitter and complex year. It ended with the first overt attempt by the Communist establishment to split the Western peace movement and bring a part of it within their control.

The attempt was signalled in a letter from Yuri Zhukov, President of the Soviet Peace Committee (December 2, 1982) which came through the postboxes of dozens of Western peace organisations and individuals. In July 1982, largely as a result of the energetic initiatives of the Russell Peace Foundation, there had been held in Brussels a successful European Nuclear Disarmament Convention. Full rights of participation had been limited to those organisations and individuals which were signatories to the END Appeal of April 1980; but others were welcomed as observers, including representatives from the Hungarian and Romanian Peace Committees. The Soviet Peace Committee had pretended to immense insult at this procedure. How dare anyone presume to convene an anti-war conference without inviting them onto the rostrum as full plenary participants? (It was never explained why it was legitimate for the World Peace Council to convene its own affiliates and invited guests at Sofia, or at Moscow or Helsinki, but illegitimate for the supporters of the END Appeal to do the same.)

Arising from the Brussels Convention an international END Liaison Committee was established (comprising major Western peace movements) to prepare for a Second END

Convention in 1983, and an invitation was accepted from a working-group (of Greens, Social-Democrats and 'Alternative List') in West Berlin. Both CND and the British END Committee were at first unhappy about the choice of Berlin as venue, since we knew that it might arouse the Russians' susceptibilities and be regarded as a 'provocation'; but our doubts were silenced, we (and most major Western peace organisations) gave our support, and, in the event, no terrible 'provocations' took place (apart from Petra Kelly and some Greens sallying into East Berlin with 'Swords into Ploughshares' badges and 'Make Love not War' T-shirts!).

Possessed by his ideological fantasies, Mr Zhukov was determined to be thoroughly provoked, many months before the event. The choice of Berlin as venue was intended (he said) to 'resuscitate revanchist sentiments', and the very discussion of 'the German question' would 'challenge the inviolability of the post-war European frontiers'. But Zhukov's polemic took in the whole non-aligned movement. The 'true objective' of the Convention's sponsors, and of 'so-called' END, was to 'split the anti-war movement', 'infiltrate cold war elements into it', and 'push the anti-war movement off the right way': i.e. a 'united universal anti-war movement' in which the official peace committees of Warsaw bloc nations should be equal participants. No less than his fellow only-two-sidesmen, Messrs Frost and Wieseltier, Mr Zhukov was driven into a frenzy by the notion of superpower co-responsibility. The leaders of the Russell Foundation and END—

> Keep foisting on others their concept of 'equal responsibility'. We are firmly convinced that this concept is aimed at the disorientation, demobilisation and undermining of the anti-war movement, and is called upon to conceal and justify an aggressive militarist policy of the USA and NATO...
>
> It is a truly monstrous design to try and use the banner of peace in order to draw the anti-war movement into what is to all intents and purposes a 'cold war' against the public in socialist countries...

The British END Committee responded to this vitriol with a long and carefully-reasoned reply, published by END's

Secretary, Meg Beresford, in the *New Statesman*, January 21, 1983. END reassured Mr Zhukov as to Berlin 'provocations', clarified its views as to superpower co-responsibility, and discussed in detail the steady increment in SS-20s:

> We invite you to reconsider your basic premise, which is that Western weapons must be aggressive and bad whereas Soviet weapons must be defensive and good. And we invite you to turn your backs upon the futile arguments of 'balance' (which are questions for military advisors and not for peace workers) and put your faith instead in a transcontinental movement of peoples. . . It is the first responsibility of peace activists in every nation to watch and to criticise the military policies of their own nation first of all.

END went on to explain its views on the bloc division of Europe:

> Barbed wire divides not only the territories of the two blocs, there is also barbed wire in peoples' minds and hearts. The change which we work for can only come about after a preparatory process in which people on both sides come into closer communication with each other, modify their perceptions of each other, learn to tolerate differences and establish mutual trust. There can be no 'victory' of one side over the other without war. Instead, there must be a healing process. . . This cannot be done by the directives of governments (which harbour, for historical reasons, deep suspicions of each other) but only, in the first place, by direct citizens' exchanges. . .
>
> If all those whom you regard as 'anti-Soviet elements' were to be purged from the Western peace movement, then that movement would be reduced in numbers from hundreds of thousands to mere hundreds. It would be reduced to a handful of small pro-Soviet committees, without influence or independence.

END also suggested that the exchange of letters might be circulated, not only in the West, but also to supporters of the Soviet Peace Committee in the Soviet Union. After two years END is still awaiting Mr Zhukov's reply. On enquiry, it turned out that the publication of END's letter in the *New Statesman* was a 'breach of protocol', making any reply 'impossible'. (It was not explained under what protocol Mr Zhukov had circulated his own bitterly-divisive letter in the Western movement.) If NATO's missiles will be sent on their way in support of 'moral ends', the SS-20s will be sent in defence of 'protocol'.

There was, however, one novel theme in Zhukov's letter, whose significance has been growing ever since. Zhukov complained bitterly about the presence at Brussels (and expected at Berlin) of a small number of emigrees or exiles from Communist countries who had given support to the non-aligned Western movement. Ironically, Zhukov's fury was most aroused by the presence at Brussels of Dr Zhores Medvedev who, with his brother Roy, had published by far the most convincing apology for Soviet militarism in terms of reaction/response to pace-setting American innovations (see *Exterminism and Cold War*, pp. 153-174). Such exiles Zhukov described as—

> A group of people who have left their countries and have nothing in common with the struggle for peace and who, while representing nobody, are busy disseminating hostile slanderous fabrications about the foreign and home policies of their former motherland.

It is clear that this was the most sensitive issue. The END Appeal had envisaged a transcontinental movement, 'a European-wide campaign, in which every kind of exchange takes place', not only between organisations but also between individuals. We knew from the outset that this would be difficult work (when Dorothy and I visited Prague in the summer of 1980 we met with little support in those critical circles who had come to view 'peace', in the aftermath of the invasion of Afghanistan, as cynical Communist rhetoric). We also knew that unofficial citizen exchanges would be resisted woodenly by the Communist apparatus. Nevertheless, we hoped that a Western peace movement, which was unconditionally opposing additions to NATO's nuclear armoury, might succeed in opening some doors to unofficial East–West dialogue. And a few East European and Soviet citizens in exile—at first a very small number—shared our perspective and gave us their valued support.

Nothing in END's perspectives drew down upon us more scepticism or ridicule than this. At first the Western media laughed us out of court: of course no independent expressions of peace would appear in the East. Then, when such expressions did appear, we were told that these were tiny and unrepresentative (as a *Times* leader wrote, a 'barely audible echo'), and the media reported them only in terms of the harassment which they suffered and never in terms of the ideas which they promoted. In Britain the public media simply repressed all discussion of this part of our perspective —for example, my proposed Dimbleby Lecture, 'Beyond the Cold War', was cancelled—since it contradicted the 'one-sided' image which opponents of the peace movement were busily promoting. Even now (November 1984), when there are many answering voices from the East, general discussion of the perspective in the Western media remains desultory and misinformed.

My intention here is not to offer an abridged history of the independent peace movements in the East. Even though these movements are still only in their early stages, their history is complex and I have no competence as their historian.* They have not been organised or single-issue movements of the Western kind, and sometimes we are considering brief episodes (like petitions against Soviet missiles in Czechoslovakia) or the voices of individuals (such as György Konrád's *Antipolitics*). All that I can do here is illustrate the problems from examples within my own experience.

The question of independent peace expressions in the Communist states is directly related to the space which exists in these states for *any* independent expressions. This

---

* END has published several special reports: *Moscow Independent Peace Group* (1982); *The New Hungarian Peace Movement* (1982); and John Sandford, *The Sword and the Ploughshare: Autonomous Peace Initiatives in East Germany* (1983). The first two are now dated and new publications are in preparation. Also Jan Kavan and Zdena Tomin (eds.), *Voices from Prague* (Palach Press/END, 1983). The best regular coverage will be found in *END Journal* (from END, Southbank House, 12 Black Prince Road, London SE1). In the United States regular reports appear in *Nuclear Times* and *Mother Jones*, and especially in *Peace & Democracy News* and *Across Frontiers*. Christian initiatives in the East are reported regularly in the *Churches Register* (END).

lies at the heart of the world peace movement's problem. There could only be a truly two-sided movement if there were some parity of rights of expression and organisation on both sides. Which there is not. Hence we are led directly into questions of civil rights, which are the necessary precedent condition for any independent peace movement's existence. It may be possible to argue that differing social systems can peacefully co-exist; but if we are to move from this increasingly-tense condition of uneasy co-existence to a condition of active peace-*making* (or healing-process) then it is no longer possible to pretend that 'peace' and 'human rights' are not inter-related. If some Eastern 'dissidents' perceive the Western peace movement as being one-sided, it is no good our retorting that they could set this right by getting a movement going on their side also. For this could simply be to offer them a ticket to prison. Which none of us has any right to do.

But the position is not as unrelieved as this. A little space for citizen dialogue can be found, and it is our business to press more open. Professional groups, writers, Christians, physicians, cities engaged in twinning—all these have found ways to enlarge a dialogue, if not to escape from controls. And spaces have been found for some independent peace actions. In the German Democratic Republic the space was afforded by the protection of the Lutheran churches, around which the youthful 'Swords into Ploughshares' manifestations grew up. In Hungary the space for 'Dialogue' groups was found in colleges and schools, in apartments and coffee-bars. In Czechoslovakia jazz and popular music clubs have shared the aspirations of the peace movement, but the most significant space has been that which the network of civil rights supporters, Charter 77, have held open, often at the cost of their liberty or livelihood.

In 1982 these spaces began to be occupied, in direct response to the Western movement. This was perhaps the year in which 'Swords into Ploughshares' had their largest manifestations. In Czechoslovakia Charter 77 commenced a public correspondence with elements of the Western movement, a cautious exploration of views; one of their three spokespersons in that year was Ladislav Lis, who had in 1968 organised in a Prague factory an underground Communist Congress in defiance of the occupation and under the gun-barrels of Soviet tanks. Fragmentary reports began to come through of the formation of the independent Moscow Group for the Establishment of Trust between the USSR and USA. And from Hungary came a steady correspondence, much of it initiated by a history graduate, Ferenc Koszegi, a founder of the 'Dialogue' Group.

At the end of September, 1982, in response to pressing invitations, Andrew White and I went to Budapest to visit 'Dialogue'. Whatever I do I am fated to bring down on my head the abuse of the only-two-sidesmen of both sides. On this occasion I have subsequently been abused by the official Hungarian Peace Council, which put around the story that I had been offered by them the use of a public lecture-hall with every facility, but that I had rudely refused. Whereas our old acquaintance, Scott McConnell in *Commentary*, writes that 'Thompson. . . spoke before the Communist party's official peace committee, and also, at his insistence, gave the same speech to private Hungarian citizens.' Both stories are false, although Mr McConnell's is the purest fabrication. It is worth teasing out the truth of this small episode, since it reveals in miniature the difficulties of direct East/West dialogue.

At Budapest airport, and before we came through customs, we were welcomed by an affable official of the Peace Council which had only got wind of our visit a few days before. I was pressed to give a talk, in the next two or three days, in a room on the Hungarian Council's premises; I replied that I hoped that this would be possible, but that I must first consult with our hosts (the 'Dialogue' group) to find out what schedule they had arranged. It was agreed that I would call at the Council's offices the next day.

At the barrier we were met by our host, Ferenc Koszegi; and also by a friend of mine, Miklos Haraszti, a prominent 'dissident' (or constructive oppositionist), author of *A Worker in a Worker's State*. Haraszti (who was not a member of 'Dialogue') drove us to the city centre, where he left us to meet our hosts. It turned out at once that we had walked into a sensitive situation. 'Dialogue' existed to further not only direct Hungary/West communication on questions of peace, but also internal dialogue within the country: they sought to bring around the same round-table people from the official Council and the constructive opposition. They did not see themselves as 'dissidents', and were hoping to pressurise the authorities into allowing them a little legal space: perhaps a meeting-room or some share in editing a regular Bulletin.

The members and supporters of the Peace Group for Dialogue were nearly all under-25 and support extended to the 15 and 16-year-olds in the school. They had, at that time, no formal programme. They were closely informed about the Western peace movement (and monitored its publications) and the thrust of 'Dialogue' was against the ideological and security structures of the cold war: they were impatient of the formal bureaucratic structure of the official Peace Council, and wished to mount their own spontaneous actions and enter direct relations with Western peace activists. They represented a cultural or sub-political generational shift as much as a political 'position': a shift away from the apathy, materialism and cynical conformism of the post-'56 (Kadar) generation, together with a rejection of bloc thinking. The mood was that of a search for a third way among the younger European generations.

But they occupied a precarious and contested space on the edge between 'semi-legality' and 'semi-illegality'. Hungary was (and remains) the most flexible of the East European states, with a degree of toleration which her neighbours envy. An oppositional friend described the situation as one of 'civilised repression'; a more optimistic friend suggested 'incipient pluralism'. It was a fine-tuned adjustment, in which the space between legality and illegality was marked by unspoken (but well-understood) taboos. We found at once that one of the most frequent terms of political discourse was 'provocation'. A 'provocation' might be a word or action designed to push people further across the border of illegality than they wished to go. There are also certain ideological limits which may not be transgressed without 'provocation'. An important one (for peace workers) was explicit criticism of the Soviet Union (although such criticisms are nourished in most Hungarian hearts) and of the Soviet military presence in Hungary. We attended one meeting of young people where, towards the end, an older man suddenly launched into a vehement speech demanding, as a priority, the withdrawal of Soviet forces from Hungary. The young 'Dialogue' supporters at once started chatting with each other, then stood up and turned their backs on the speaker, talking to each other in groups and ignoring him. A few left the room. It was explained to us afterwards that this had been a 'provocation'. A more charitable friend suggested that the man was not a real provocateur, but one of the 'wounded' of 1956, traumatised by the experience. Yes, it was possible to discuss Soviet military withdrawal in Hungary; but only in the context of a transcontinental peace movement, making equal demands upon both sides.

The presence of these taboos can be felt as an invisible but palpable element in every discourse, defining the limits of the possible. Indeed, the ruling authorities are well aware of this, and use it as a means of intellectual and social control. Even in discussions with official persons one may be told, in a man-to-man, 'off-the-record' sort of way, that Hungary is a small and weak country with powerful neighbours, and regrettably the limits of any autonomy are strictly confined. The legacy of 1956 still hangs over all discourse.

At certain points the space between legality and illegality is more clearly defined. Two limitations are of particular importance: (1) the prohibition of illegal publishing, or *samizdat;* (2) the prohibition of unauthorised but publicly advertised open political meetings. Even here there are nuances. A good deal of *samizdat* is in wide circulation. Carbons circulate normally among friends. (By contrast, in Romania typewriters must be registered with the authorities as if they were hand-guns). There was even, in 1982, a *samizdat* 'bookshop' open every Tuesday evening in the centre of Budapest. The shop was in fact the apartment of Laszlo Rajk, an architect, whose father (also Laszlo) was a leader of the Hungarian Communist Party who had been executed after World War II after one of the notorious Stalinist show-trials. When Andrew and I visited the 'shop' we found that a new *samizdat* pamphlet was being published that day—a translation of my own not-the-Dimbleby-lecture, 'Beyond the Cold War'. It seems that the lecture was no more acceptable to the Communist authorities than it had been to the BBC.

Of course, visitors to the 'bookshop' were noticed: there was a plain-clothes man at the foot of the apartment stairs. Every now and then the shop would be raided and some *samizdat* confiscated. But it was a harassment which stopped short of serious repression. There were similar nuances with respect to meetings. Small discussion groups in private homes were going on all the time, and they still are. They are a normal mode of discourse and not the cloak-and-dagger affairs of Western imagination. We attended such local meetings of Dialogue supporters, where a dozen or so students and senior school pupils discussed international questions without inhibition or anxiety. Such meetings would cross the line to semi-illegality only if they were conducted 'provocatively' or raised 'provocative' questions. Those who crossed this line were rarely subjected to direct repressive measures. The authorities employed the stick and the carrot in more subtle ways. People could lose their jobs or job opportunities or their right to travel. Their post could be interfered with, although not by the brutal confiscations frequent in Czechoslovakia and the USSR. This was already going on around us. One 'Dialogue' member had unexpectedly been called up for military service; the homes of secondary school students active in Dialogue had been visited by security officers, to the consternation of their parents; teachers had issued warnings. In 1983 all this was to increase.

But in September 1982 Dialogue occupied a semi-legal space. Their activities were completely open ('we insist on acting as free persons', one of the founders, Ferenc Ruzsa, said), and they were in open negotiation with the Peace Council. But they could not hire public rooms, nor advertise meetings in the press, nor publish any literature. Even the beautiful badge which they designed, the CND sign in the form of clasped hands holding a rose, in the Hungarian colours, could not be manufactured in Hungary. (Andrew and I brought the design back, END manufactured them, and subsequent visitors took badges across—until the authorities denounced this as 'foreign intervention' and Dialogue replaced them with paper stick-ons of their own manufacture.) They could run off a couple of dozen typed carbon copies of their own internal bulletin, but they refused to cross the legality border to real *samizdat.* The art students could use silk screens and designed beautiful posters. This, and the telephone, and the word-of-mouth message, comprised their resources.

It was into this narrow space that we blundered, bringing messages of goodwill from END and from branches of CND. We were among the earlier visitors to Dialogue and very many were to follow. We found at once that the question of my 'lecture' had acquired symbolic significance. Permission had been given to Dialogue to use a lecture-theatre at Budapest University, but a day or two before my arrival permission had been withdrawn. It was 'known', but could not be proved, that pressure had been brought to bear from outside the University, perhaps because such a lecture, under Dialogue auspices, was felt to be offensive to the Peace Council whose prerogative it was to be the sole conduit for Western peace visitors.

My hosts were, not surprisingly, angry that the lecture-theatre had been cancelled. They saw the invitation to me to speak on Peace Council premises as an attempt to co-opt me into that operation. Publicity for this in the press or on television would be a defeat for Dialogue; the average TV viewer, in any case, would turn the telly off with a yawn, saying: 'Oh, someone else getting a free trip!' In Dialogue's view, my agreement to take part in a round-table or meeting on Peace Council premises should be conditional upon my obtaining permission to lecture also in public, hosted by Dialogue. It was explained to me that not many young people would dream of going to a meeting at the Peace Council anyway, since the whole set-up was so stuffy.

There commenced two days of strenuous negotiations with the Peace Council. I had no objection to speaking on Council premises, provided that the other condition could be met. END, like CND, has always been in favour of plural exchanges: that is, we should speak with whomsoever, official or unofficial, is willing to speak with us, whether in the East or West. Critics of the peace movement have strange double-standards: when Mrs Thatcher speaks at an official banquet in Budapest, she is hailed as a far-sighted proponent of. . . 'dialogue' (a term which the young Dialogue group first brought back into political discourse): when a peace worker speaks on the other side, s/he is written off as a 'useful idiot' or pro-Soviet toad. However, I do consider it important when we visit the other side that we should speak firmly and explicitly in criticism of the militarism of both blocs, and should insist on speaking with whomsoever we choose.

My negotiations in this case culminated in a meeting in a cafe with several officials of the Peace Council. It was a discussion conducted with courtesy and over several beers. I was warmly invited to give my lecture on the Peace Council's premises, before an invited audience with representatives of the churches, scientists and youth. Perhaps a larger room could be found, and more youth could be invited. Some members of Dialogue would be invited too. I explained, frankly and courteously, the principles of a non-aligned movement: I would be happy to give the lecture, but I must also lecture publicly under the auspices of my hosts in Dialogue. Why not in the University? But (it turned out) the university authorities were 'autonomous' and it would be improper for the Peace Council to seek to influence them. Perhaps (I suggested) the Ministry of the Interior might have influenced the University? But the Ministry of the Interior (it turned out) was 'autonomous' also, and the Peace Council could not influence it. It transpired that the Secretary of the Council had been trying all day to book a public meeting-hall for me, perhaps a trade-union hall; but (surprise) every hall in Budapest was booked that night. After all, it was not usual that foreign tourists should arrive one day and demand a lecture-hall the next—how would we feel if they were to arrive in London with such a demand? More beer. Every now and then the conversation would shift to other matters—general peace policy—and I would find that it was somehow assumed that I had agreed to their proposals. When I dug in my heels, the offers went up. The lecture, on their premises, would be publicly advertised: the text would be published: I might have a slot on Hungarian peak television and address 10 million Hungarians, direct and uncensored. What I could not do was hold a public meeting under the auspices of Dialogue. In the end they realised that I could not change this condition. They were good and courteous losers, and invited me to lunch the next day. The lunch was excellent and the discussion frank.

Our hosts in Dialogue had therefore to accept the cancellation of the lecture or look for alternative private premises. Several sympathisers with large apartments were approached but without success. Finally, on two hours' notice, an invitation was received from György Konrád, one of Hungary's leading novelists, of the hospitality of his apartment. The invitation was accepted, perhaps a little grudgingly, because Konrád is known as a constructive oppositionist. In some miraculous ways the news of the venue was passed from mouth to mouth, and when we arrived some eighty young people were packed into two adjoining rooms. It was a deeply-serious, positive and responsive audience.

I have written out this small episode in such detail because it illustrates the complexities and tensions of opening direct dialogue on the other side. Very many other Western peace workers have had similar experiences, not only in Hungary but also (in different conditions) in Poland or the GDR or even the USSR. Always there is the polarisation between the official structures legitimated by the Party, on one hand, and 'dissidents' on the other, and always there is the difficulty of speaking with both (e.g. with the Soviet Peace Committee and the Moscow Trust Group) or of finding intermediate spaces in the tug-of-war between. For a brief period Hungarian Dialogue and the GDR 'Swords into Ploughshares' were remarkable in opening up a hitherto impossible space for semi-legal political autonomy from the 'leading role' of the Communist Party. They were able to do so, perhaps, because their function (as a peace movement) was not seen to be threatening, and because the Western peace movement afforded some small protection. It may also be that Dialogue was protected by 'doves' in the Party itself, who favoured a little pluralism; while the Hungarian Peace Council is the most flexible and well-informed of any in the Warsaw bloc.

The space opened up by Dialogue was an uneasy one. I noted two contrasting comments made at the time. The first was from a 'dissident' or democratic oppositionist:

> The Western peace movements make a great mistake when they enter into relations with official Peace Committees in the attempt to influence them or to use them as a channel to reach the public. In fact, these official bodies stand in the space where, otherwise, an independent peace movement would spring up. Their function is that of inhibiting the development of an independent movement, or of controlling it if it should begin to arise. Every Western visit to, or acknowledgement of, the official committees in fact legitimises their function of the repression of true peace movements.

The other comment came from a leading member of Dialogue:

> The official Peace Council wishes to do one or the other of two things. It wishes either to co-opt us (while allowing us a little space, a little flexibility within their control) or, if it cannot do that, then it wishes to drive us into 'opposition'. They are afraid of our influence so long as we are 'semi-legal': we can then reach a wide public, especially in the schools. But if we are driven into 'semi-illegality' (with the use of *samizdat*, etc.) then we may remain a small intellectual force: but they can isolate us from the general public. The teachers and (even more) the parents will bring pressure on the school students. Our problem is this: the oppositionists want to provoke us into opposition, and the authorities (if they cannot control us) want to do the same.

For many months the 'semi-legal' space was held open—and it rapidly enlarged. Dialogue soon had thousands of supporters and groups grew up in the provinces. Many Western peace activists were received with unfailing generosity by Dialogue hosts. The Hungarian authorities then, and (with several sad exceptions) since, have treated these visitors with propriety and courtesy, and have let us talk with whom we wished. The Peace Council, while sometimes grumpy, has maintained formal courtesies, and has made an in-put into END Conventions. On several occasions Western peace visitors—Mary Kaldor, the editor of *END Journal*, Mient-Jan Faber and others from the Dutch IKV, Stephen Tunnicliffe, the editor of *END Churches Register*—were able to engage in 'trialogues', in which they discussed with both 'officials' and 'independents' around the same table.

But the tension expressed in the two contrasting comments above exerted itself relentlessly and, in the end, it pulled Dialogue apart. By the summer of 1983 the 'semi-legal' space had almost closed. For the young actors in these disputes it seemed that the splits in Dialogue were the result of their own internal dissensions; there have been (alas!) accusations and counter-accusations of bad faith. Yet as is so often the case, internal dissension was the product of external pressures which, at the time, they could not clearly see. A major pressure was that, from the first days of 1983, to re-establish 'the leading role of the Party' throughout the Warsaw bloc; not only Solidarnosc but also the spread of the Western peace infection into the East was to be controlled. Eager cold warriors in the West, in Radio Free Europe etc., acted as 'mixers' by issuing selective and sensational reports in which Dialogue was assimilated to 'dissidents'. Perhaps one or two Western free-lance peace visitors (but not, I think, from Britain) helped this confusion on. Mr Zhukov's letter (above p. 55) and the argument surrounding the rival Berlin and Prague conferences introduced new tensions. It is probable that 'the Russians' leaned on the Hungarian authorities. It is now known (for documents fall off the back of lorries in Budapest as well as Whitehall) that the Politbureau of the Hungarian Socialist Workers (Communist) Party accepted a report, at its meeting on March 29th, 1983, which signalled that it would no longer tolerate the semi-legal status of Dialogue.

This report spells out very clearly the mentalities and

methods of Party authoritarianism and deserves careful attention. Those who do not understand these methods of social regulation and intellectual control will always be innocents in their relations with official Peace Councils. The report was drawn up by the Central Committee Section for Party and Mass Organisations. It commenced by commenting on the 'new phenomenon' of 'efforts towards spontaneous peace movements', and upon the need to 'develop united political behaviour' in relation to this phenomenon. The influence upon Hungarian opinion of the 'large and multi-coloured mass actions' of Western peace movements, with their opposition to the 'superpowers', was noted. This influence had been felt especially among Hungarian youth, who were attracted by 'more colourful and lively forms' of action. As a result, several spontaneous initiatives had taken place, culminating in the Dialogue groups:

> The group does not have any significant mass support, but its influence is growing. At the present moment Dialogue groups are operating in Budapest, Szeged, Debrecen and Pécs. Their ideas are in equal measure mixed, immature and self-contradictory, even giving rise to controversy in their own circles. . . Pacifist efforts. . . in church and religious circles are also on the increase.

While the National Peace Council had tried to monitor and maintain contacts with such groups, 'a united standpoint' had not yet been formed as to how to handle them. 'The Party organs have not everywhere paid sufficient attention to directing and supervising the peace movement,' and the Peace Council had 'not been able to integrate the spontaneous peace initiatives within the bounds of their own framework.' Moreover, oppositional groups had sought to make use of these groups in order to strengthen their own influence and to encourage 'so-called independent forces outside the Party and state'. The demand for a nuclear-free Europe could also be a form of disguised 'anti-Sovietism'.

While the report noted that Dialogue had held itself distinct from oppositional groups, nevertheless 'their activities are not free from oppositional influences'.

> In the name of the 'independent Hungarian peace movement' they build up foreign connections, invite foreign guests, and organise forums for them. They popularise their viewpoints in duplicated publications. According to these, they place equal responsibility for the intensification of the arms race on the United States of America and the Soviet Union. They do not believe in the possibility of success in disarmament negotiations carried on between governments. It is their belief that only the building up of a broad popular movement and the exercise of pressure on governments can lead to results.

They support the aims of END, and END 'supports them materially as well*. . .' This causes problems for the foreign contacts of the National Peace Council. The report concluded that it was necessary to enliven the routine and stereotyped forms of agitation available to the youth, and raise the level of their political understanding.

The Political Committee of the Communist Party, having frowned for a while over this report, came up with a series of Resolutions. It was decreed that where any form of peace group (clubs, debating forums, youth committees) came into existence, measures should be taken to 'ensure that they are brought into connection with the united movement directed by the National Peace Council'. It was also advised that 'their operations be tied to the places of work and institutions of education' (i.e. they should not function without supervision in apartments, coffee-bars and clubs). 'The responsible and orderly political orientation of these groups—by their activists—is the task of the Party and social organs and organisations in the workplace.'

At the same time, Party activists 'should expose and isolate in open debate' all those using the peace movement 'as a pretext for questioning the peace policies of our Party and Government, our commitments to our allies, and the initiatives for peace of the Soviet Union'. And—

> If the activities of the groups comes into conflict with the law, if they offend against the fundamental principles of our state, then

* i.e. in making the first Dialogue badges—the only material aid that END ever gave!

> **administrative methods should also be used. . . The Hungarian peace movement must be kept united under the direction of the National Peace Council. Movements standing outside the Peace Council cannot be legalised.**

For the rest, the Political Committee supported more colourful efforts to organise demonstrations, marches, debating forums, etc., 'appropriate to political needs, and. . . serving the social base of the foreign policy decisions of our government'. On these occasions 'it considers it necessary' that the Peace Council and the Communist Youth League (KISZ) 'should provide the badges, placards and other symbols. . . for youth peace actions'. Nothing, absolutely nothing, could be left unprovided-for by the all-wise guidance of the Party Central Committee and its handmaiden, the Peace Council. The brief era of spontaneity must be brought to a close.*

Under such pressures Dialogue came apart. The authorities withdrew the carrot and made more use of the stick. A crisis was reached in late July 1983 when a number of Western visitors arrived to take part in a summer peace camp arranged by Dialogue; at the last moment camp-sites were refused, and after some tense and confused discussions in Budapest, the police arrested many visitors (including four women from the Greenham Peace Camp) and ushered them roughly across the border. (Dr Lynne Jones wrote a lucid account of the whole episode in the *Guardian*, August 4th, 1983.) This introduced a heavier climate of somewhat less civilised repression; harassments, detentions, a few fines. In a separate incident the *samizdat* publisher, Gabor Demszky, was beaten up by plain-clothes police, and then charged with assault. Although the trial ended in a suspended sentence, it was the first trial of an opposition figure for some years. I mention it here, because Dr Demszky had published the *samizdat* of my own 'Beyond the Cold War'. Laszlo Rajk's *samizdat* 'bookshop' has also been closed down.

This is only a small part of a much fuller history, which is continuing and will be continued, since the Hungarian peace

* These documents were first published in *Alulnézet Kiadó* (Bottom-View Publishers), a *samizdat* publishing-house in Budapest, 1984.

movement is only in its earlier stages.* What used to be Dialogue split into two wings; those who, with Koszegi, chose legality at the cost of some independence, founding a new club in semi-detached relation to the Peace Council; and those who opted for *samizdat* and semi-illegality, which brought them into closer relations with those democratic oppositionists (such as Haraszti, Rajk and others) who also wish to be in dialogue with the Western peace movement. In between, fragments of semi-legal Dialogue continue to meet, and to welcome Western visitors; although some lost heart and dropped into inactivity.†

A similar account might be given of the complexities of dialogue with the independent peace forces in the GDR. What needs to be stressed, in both cases, is that while there have been great difficulties in maintaining autonomous organisational identities, the general *peace culture* (especially among young people) continues to grow. It is inevitable that new forms of expression will be found. And the search for these forms must be carried out by the citizens of these nations alone. It is no business of Western activists to interfere in any way in these internal affairs, or to seek to import their own prescriptions. Any such attempts will, anyway, be counter-productive. Since there is a small percentage of individualists, know-alls and nutters among Western visitors, some of them have tried and, no doubt, will continue to try to interfere.

It is also always possible (and in some future situations might even become probable) that other, more noisome, agents might try to play a hand in the same game. Just as Mr Zhukov and his friends view the Western peace movement in terms of an opportunity to exploit a 'weakness' within

* In the foregoing account I am much indebted to END's Hungary working group, to Hugh Baldwin's monitoring of the Hungarian press, and to information from friends in Hungary.

† An important example of the space still held open for 'third way' peace initiatives has been the informal seminar, 'Towards a Theology of Peace', held in Budapest in September 1984, jointly organised by Bishop Karoly Tóth of the Hungarian Reformed Church and Stephen Tunnicliffe, coordinator of END Churches Lateral Committee, and attended by Christians from thirty countries, East, West and Third World: see *END Churches Register*, Autumn 1984.

NATO to the advantage of the Warsaw bloc, so their *alter egos* in the Western war movement will view independent peace expressions in the East as opportunities to 'de-stabilise' the other side to Western advantage.

Mr George Urban, from his position of influence as Director of Radio Free Europe, has recently argued—

> Let us look at the chances of weakening the Soviet system in peaceable ways. . . Don't you think we could export, or re-export, this propagandist obsession with 'peace' to the Soviet Union and its client states in Eastern Europe? Couldn't we tell the Ukrainians, for example, that the deployment of so many Russian missiles on their soil would do nothing for their survival in a nuclear war—exactly as the Soviet Marshals are telling West Germany? Can you envisage Ukrainian 'peace'-marchers parading in the streets of Kiev under posters reading 'Ukrainian mothers will not allow their sons to die for Andropov's war', or 'KGB cooks books to exaggerate US nuclear arsenal'?. . . Couldn't we gently remind them through our information services: 'You may find yourselves in extreme danger if a nuclear war should break out. . . Show your national independence by demanding the removal of foreign rockets—and stay alive'? (*Encounter*, May 1984).

These are interesting questions when posed by a director of one of 'our information services'. It reminds one that not everything that Mr Zhukov says about NATO's psychological war agencies is rubbish. How much of this is now being done? Which of us, in the Western peace movement, monitor Radio Free Europe, Radio Liberty, and the Voice of America? Or even the BBC Russian Service? It is for reasons such as this that some in the West have come to view with extreme caution independent expressions from the East. Are they genuine? Might they not be one of Mr Urban's 'plants'?

I can offer no easy answers. There may be 'plants', on that side as on this. There may also be cases where authentic centres of 'dissidence' employ the rhetoric of 'peace' as a cover for the pursuit of other oppositional objectives. Our amateur movement, with its slender resources, must find its way to friends in the East blindfold and tapping a white stick. We can only act as Dialogue commenced to act, as 'free persons', accepting dialogue when it is offered, refusing any methods of conspiracy, arguing the issues openly, making our judgments as we go along. Sometimes we may find that we must risk an act of faith—or trust.

This was, exactly, the case with the Moscow Trust Group. Some circumstances surrounding the group's origin seemed curious. Its existence was first announced at the time that the Scandinavian Women's Peacemarch was about to enter the Soviet Union. Could a small 'dissident' peace group be an exercise in cold war propaganda? Reports and the group's early statements came mainly through Western correspondents in Moscow. But, then, how else were they to get any messages out? Then Danielle Grünberg, a West Country member of CND of Danish extraction (the only Briton on the Scandinavian march) took her trust in her hands and (with Jean Stead of the *Guardian*) visited the Trust Group—she was the only marcher to do so, and she deserves our thanks. Danielle's and Jean's reports were positive; so also were reports from other American and British peace workers who visited the group, and who came to know the members' views and circumstances. One remarkable American visitor even managed to visit the group's founder, the young artist Sergei Batovrin, when he was placed in a psychiatric hospital. Meanwhile news of the group's harassment became worse and worse. They were accused by the Soviet authorities (and the Soviet Peace Committee) of being 'hooligans' and 'drunkards' and 'Zionists' (some of them are Jews) or 'refuseniks' seeking tickets to the West (some of the group's founders had filed applications to emigrate, but, on the foundation of the group, several had withdrawn their applications).

END decided to trust the Trust Group: that is, we decided, not that the group was a like-minded group which shared our strategies, but that it was a group of independent-minded and courageous persons, deeply-concerned about peace, in a situation of extreme exposure which demanded some solidarity from the Western movement. We therefore published an *END Special Report* which included press reports, some statements of the group, and the accounts of Danielle Grünberg and Jean Stead. It was the first substantial English-language publicity for the group's existence, and it carried the information widely into Europe and the USA. This pamphlet, and supporting representations and letters in the press, may have done a little to offer protection to the group, and even to get Batovrin out of psychiatric detention. It was an action which drew upon END the particular hostility of the Soviet Peace Committee, which found its legitimacy to be challenged by the group's existence.

It was an action which also met with some scepticism in the peace movement, and among our own supporters. Although we made it clear that we did not (and do not) regard the Trust Group as the only locus for dialogue with Soviet citizens—and continue to favour an extensive plural dialogue—we were accused of identifying with a small group of unrepresentative 'dissidents', who might even have been 'set up' to embarrass the Soviet authorities.

It was at this time, when some of us in END and CND were making representations on behalf of the group—in the face of much scepticism—that we were hit amidships by the Popov missile. To our astonishment there surfaced briefly in London a Dr Oleg Popov, who pronounced himself to be the authorised 'spokesman' of the group in the West, who gave interviews in several national newspapers, had instant access to the news programmes of the BBC, and who signed a letter (drafted by other hands) in *The Times.* In these Dr Popov said nothing about the policies of the Trust Group, nothing about its activities but much about its harassment and repression, and delivered his condemnation (in the name of the Trust Group) of any 'unilateral' measures and especially of the policies of END, CND and the Labour Party. His views of the prospects for the Trust Group were profoundly pessimistic ('under the existing power structure in the Soviet Union' there was almost no hope of building an independent peace movement, and the support of Western 'unilateralist groups has proved to be in vain', *Times*, November 8, 1982), and he wrote (or someone wrote and he signed) that 'we do not want our existence to be exploited by bodies of unilateralists who do not share our aims'.

This was a most damaging attack, and its ill effects can be felt in the British peace movement to this day. They may also have been felt in Moscow. As Dorothy and I wrote, in a response in *The Times* (November 17th): 'Does Dr Popov not know that he has given a licence to the KGB to portray the Moscow Group as nothing but a Western intelligence "plant", drawing in a few innocent persons, whose ulterior aim was to discomfort Western peace movements?' There are some in the Western peace movement who still feel that, having burnt their fingers trying to support the Moscow Trust Group, they will never risk burning their fingers with independent movements in the East again.

Who was Dr Oleg Popov? He was not a member of the Trust Group, but he was friendly with several members, was one among several score of signatories to the group's first Appeal (June 2nd, 1982), and gave the group some advice as to its legal status. He was not its official 'spokesman' in the West, but when he received emigration papers from the Soviet Union a few weeks after the Group's foundation (in July) he was asked to take messages out. He came by way of Vienna to Italy, and in early November was flown for three or four days to London to consult with Amnesty International on matters concerning the persecution of the Moscow Helsinki Group. By then he was completely out of touch with the Trust Group, and at that time some of us in the British and American peace movements were in more direct communication. He knew nothing about Britain, nor about the representations made on the Trust Group's behalf by END and CND (Bruce Kent had spoken out publicly in Moscow in its defence).

At the time there were deep suspicions about Popov; but I now consider that his offence was weakness—he blundered into a situation he did not understand and allowed himself to be made use of by others. This view is the charitable one taken by members of the Moscow Trust Group itself. Several members wrote to me next February apologising for

> our friend Oleg Popov. There is no doubt that he acted with insufficient tact, publicly expressing his views about END without meeting you first. . . It can only be justified by explaining that the psychological strain connected with emigration, adapting to sharply different conditions of life and finally, a lack of knowledge of the

traditions and ways of life in the West placed him in a very difficult position. . .

They add that if they had agreed with Dr Popov's assertion that 'under the existing power structure in the Soviet Union' there could be no hope of independent peace initiatives, then 'it goes without saying that we would never have entered the Trust Group'.

Oleg Popov, having unloosed his missile, flew back to Italy, and thence onward to the United States, where he has been rather quiet about Trust Group matters. He does not appear on the editorial board of *Return Address: Moscow*, the English-language bulletin of Group members in exile. If we wished to tease out the true details of this operation we would have to examine certain little offices in London to which Dr Popov was introduced, as the supposed offices of multilateral 'disarmament' movements: the Coalition for Peace through Security, which specialises in dirty tricks against CND, and the office in Golden Square which houses (surprise, surprise!) the pretentiously-named Institute for European Defence and Strategic Studies of Mr Gerald Frost (above p. 3). At this same address were then to be found a number of peace-loving organisations, including the Institute for the Study of Conflict, Alliance Publishers, the Anglo-Russian Peace Movement and the Association for a Free Russia. This well-funded operation (END could not dream of renting premises in Golden Square nor employing telex and half-a-dozen typists) is not—as one visitor remarked—exactly a hole in the wall. It appears to have the best of connections with like-minded organisations, including the Coalition for Peace through Security, some services of the BBC, and *Encounter*. Its credentials as the office of mass movements are less secure: the 'Anglo-Russian Peace Movement', set up after Dr Popov's visit and perhaps now defunct, is supposed to have had three members, two of whom were Young Conservatives who had distinguished themselves in a heroic operation running up and down a Moscow underground distributing leaflets hidden in their socks.

It was to this honeypot that Oleg Popov was directed, and

there are other such honeypots in the West. I will be frank and admit that, when Sergei Batovrin and his family were (in effect) expelled from the Soviet Union at the end of May 1983, Dorothy and I flew to Vienna not only to welcome them with flowers but also to forestall another Popov operation. We need not have worried, since Sergei already had some notion of what to expect in the West. The Batovrins moved on to New York, where they continue to work for Trust, produce a journal, and are in continuous discussions with the American peace movement. The egregious Gerald Frost, of Golden Square, keeps jumping up and down in *Encounter* (May 1984 and 'Letters', July/August 1984) proclaiming that I have misrepresented Sergei Batovrin's views for malign purposes. He wishes to persuade readers of *Encounter* that Batovrin is (like Dr Popov) contemptuous of the Western peace movement and has lost interest in conducting any dialogue or joint actions with its members.

This is far from the truth. Batovrin and a small group of his fellow-exiles in New York are now very active in publicising the cause of the Trust Group in the Western peace movement. Their journal (*Return Address: Moscow*) is sharp in tone, and may be criticised for giving more publicity to KGB harassment than to the positive work and proposals of the group. And it has been so criticised. No doubt there may be differences of view in Trust Group circles (both in Moscow and abroad), as are commonly found in such situations. But it is, most emphatically, Batovrin's intention to strengthen direct East-West citizen communication, even if at the painful cost of destroying some Western illusions.

In any case, Batovrin has never asked Frost to be his amanuensis, nor has he invited me. He is perfectly capable of correcting either one of us if he so wishes. When he came through England in October 1984 to do a series of meetings with the peace movement (some of them hosted by END) he made none of the complaints which Mr Frost seeks to put into his mouth. It is also instructive to note that—although a press release was put out by END in good time—the only national paper to notice his visit was the *Guardian*, while both BBC and ITV turned down opportunities for interviews. It seems that most of the media are interested in Russian peaceniks only if they come, like Oleg Popov, with missiles to launch at CND and END.

Dr Popov's complaint was against 'unilateralists' who do not share the Trust Group's aims. Of course, no-one ever has supposed or said that the group supported 'unilateralism'. Their position on nuclear weapons is similar to that of many in the American movement: they support a freeze and mutual balanced reductions. They do not criticise Soviet armaments policies (such criticism would anyway be a legal offence). This being so, they do not assume the right to criticise the armaments policies of other nations either. As a point of principle, their proposals are always framed as positive suggestions rather than as criticisms. Several of them have written to us privately, expressing courteous doubts as to the advisability of a British policy of unilateral nuclear disarmament. But we have never been able to have a thorough discussion of these questions, simply because the Soviet security authorities have always made the exchange of letters, books and documents so difficult.

However, the question of 'unilateralism' is beside the point. We never supported the rights of the Trust Group on the grounds that they endorsed our policies, nor have they asked us to endorse theirs. We simply supported their right to exist and to do their own thing, and to contribute in this way to the common dialogue. This is also the way in which Professor Yuri Medvedkov saw it, in an early letter to END (December 29, 1982):

> It is up to us (participants of the independent peace movements) to provide alternative forms of constructive East-West dialogue. . . There is some division of labour among various peace movements. . . For the public of Western nations it is permitted to object to budgetary appropriations and to political alliances of certain kinds. As for the Trust-Building Group, the field of vision plus the field of possibilities both dictate the emphasis on steps for healthier detente, with our conviction that it's not weapons but people with hatred who do the killing.

(*END Journal*, 2, Feb.-March 1983).

This has always been the emphasis of the Trust Group's work, and it is this which the Western movement has learned from them and should go on learning. While the Western activists have been preoccupied with the build-up of nuclear weapons (and the West's prior responsibility in this), the Trust Group has been preoccupied with distrust and ideological confrontation (and their own authorities' responsibility in this), and they have issued proposal after proposal for greater citizen exchange. In this they have shown astonishing courage. As Yuri Medvedkov wrote: 'We risk our liberty and even our lives every day, but to be outside the peace movement is impossible for us. It's the point of honour, the point of being humans.'

In the past two years I have accumulated enough files on the Moscow Trust Group to write a fat book. These include letters and proposals from the group, furious attacks from the Soviet Peace Committee, the records of disputes in the Western movement, and reports of the growing number of Western peace visitors to the group—the important visits of Women for Life on Earth (who took Olga Medvedkova with them into the innermost sanctum of the Soviet Peace Committee), of the American Friends Service Committee, of members of CND and European peace organisations. But even if I were to write this book, I do not know what I would say in the conclusion. Perhaps this may be because the story is not yet concluded.

What I have learned is something of the complexity of attempting an independent initiative in the capital city of the Soviet Union; the fierce loyalty of the group's members to each other, but also their fierce disputes and divisions. Although I have never visited Russia, I have come to know the members as neighbours and friends. I have known of their moments of despair and also of renewed hope. I have also learned of the impossible pressures placed upon them—not only the surveillance, the house arrests, the telephones cut, the interrogations, the exhibitions and paintings confiscated, the slanders in the press, the arrests and emigration of members, the suspicion of neighbours—but also the repeated confusions as to direction, the suspicion of penetration (might someone be an informer? and to the KGB or to Western intelligence?), the succession of Western visitors expecting immediate attention—many of them true-hearted and welcome, but a few false-hearted ones trying to trick them into 'provocations' on one side or the other in the Cold War. And, on the bottom line, moments of black pessimism when members of the group have come to doubt the very purpose of their work. Might it not be that, by becoming the occasion for a 'cold war' within the peace movements, they might actually be worsening 'trust'? 'We appeal to you' (one of them wrote to me in September 1984) 'not to make any actions with the goal of helping us, if such actions could seriously deteriorate international relations. Peace is more important than our lives. . .'

Not once but several hundred times I have been told that the group may be very 'sincere' but that they are a tiny group of unrepresentative intellectuals (or Jews or refuseniks) who are a distraction to the business of making peace with Soviet people. Not once but a dozen times something odd has happened which has made me wonder if there was not some cold war joker in the Trust Group pack. Not once but twenty times it would have been easy to throw all the papers in the air and to walk out of the room. But I am glad that many of us—and now an increasing number—answered the group with our own trust. If we had not stood by those beleaguered people it would have been an act of such deep dishonour that it would have called the whole project of the Western peace movement in question.

If the independent peace movement in the GDR and in Hungary has acted always in a narrow and precarious space, any independent group in the USSR acts in no space at all. Its space is a small apartment under surveillance, and even the visitors may only be wearing masks of goodwill. The two 'sides' press almost physically upon them, and any third way of peace is disallowed by the rules of state. The very act of existence is construed as a 'provocation', which is regarded with particular fury by the official Peace Committee since it feels that its own legitimacy is called in question. However much the group proclaims that it is not 'dissident', the KGB uses every means to try and drive it into dissident mentalities.

The Trust Group took the sharpest action possible, by just existing, by publicly proclaiming its own existence, and by entering into open communication with Westerners. Was it wise to do so? Were there intermediate ways, which others have been quietly taking? I do not know. But in doing so, it broke, not this specific law or that (for the group has always sought to assert only its legal rights), but the dominant taboo of the Soviet state: the leading role of the Party—and this in the most sensitive ideological area. We can illustrate this by examining some extraordinary documents which dropped off the back of a lorry in Siberia.*

The documents refer to Alexander Shatravka, a supporter of the Trust Group with a 'dissident' record: he had suffered previous imprisonment for attempting to cross the border into Finland. He was an early signatory to the group's Appeal of June 4, 1982, and he took the Appeal with him on a trip into Siberia, collecting signatures in villages and at a sawmill. He was arrested, tried, and sentenced to three years in a Siberian labour camp. He succeeded in appealing, and the case was referred to the Procuracy of the city of Tyumen.

I have before me an incomplete record of the examination. The case turned on the question of the Trust Group's founding Appeal, and whether this was or was not an infringement of Soviet law. This document was examined by several learned Thebans, and their opinions were given. First, Dr Woldemar Alekseyevich Danilov, assistant professor of history and dean of the History Faculty of Tyumen State University, found that the document was of an 'anti-Soviet, anti-Socialist character', bearing 'a pacifist character'. Among its offences were that 'it posits equality between the positions and aims of the USSR and USA', 'there is an attempt to underestimate the significance of contemporary forms of the movement of peace champions', and 'the idea is expressed of the formation of some kind of public force, standing above governments', an idea which reflects 'cosmo-

---

* I am indebted to Sergei Batovrin for copies, and to Gerard Holden for the translations which follow, as well as for advice on other points in this essay.

politan ideas'. The Trust Group's Appeal 'could give rise to incorrect ideas, especially among that part of the population which is not well-prepared politically'. Thus the learned Dr Danilov. His colleague, Gennady Filippovich Kutsev, Rector of the same University, concurred: the document expressed 'the well-known thesis of Western propaganda concerning the equal responsibility of imperialist and socialist countries for the cold war. . .' Dr Kutsev noted that appropriate scientific specialists were already handling Soviet disarmament negotiations: 'it should however be noted that modern weapons systems are so complex that in practice it is impossible and even unwise to bring unprepared people into the consideration of these problems'.

Reinforced by these expert legal opinions, the Procuracy got down to a formal judicial examination before a Commission comprised of Professor G.B. Ignatenko, head of the Law Department at the R.D. Rudenko Institute; Professor K.N. Lyubishin, Ph.D., head of the History and Philosophy Department at the Ural State University; and Professor G.P. Orlov, Ph.D., head of 'historical materialism' at the same University. This Commission 'established' a number of points. The Appeal of the Trust Group was 'naive', 'utopian' and 'slanderous'. It was also 'directly opposed to the essence of Marxist–Leninist ideology'. After much rehearsal of these themes the Commission came to judgment. According to article 62 of the Soviet Constitution citizens 'are obliged to defend the interests of the Soviet state, to assist the strengthening of its power and authority'. Those who drew up the Appeal had broken this 'constitutional norm'. And in accordance with article 190 of the criminal code of the Russian Soviet Federal Socialist Republic 'it is not necessary to establish actual consequences'. Intention or 'purpose' was decisive. And the Appeal had two such hostile purposes. First, internally, it attempted to set society in opposition to the Soviet state and Party and 'place them in a position of mutual antagonism', by setting up spontaneous national groups with international contacts.

'The call to unite international social groups* is nothing other than a call for the formation of a group of "initiators" outsite the framework of our state.' Second, externally,

> The outward orientation is a weakening of the position of Soviet diplomacy in the negotiations in progress, to the detriment of the authority of the Soviet leadership in the eyes of *those international forces which are considered by us, and can practically be used as, an effective reserve in the anti-imperialist and anti-militarist struggle*. . . [My italics—*E.P.T.*]

Finally, the Appeal's 'call for the provision of "free" information about disarmament on both sides about the deployment of armaments† is equivalent to an intention to reveal Soviet defence capabilities to a potential aggressor'.

Thus refreshed, these learned Thebans no doubt returned to their rigorous academic studies of law and historical materialism. Alexander Shatravka returned to his labour camp. Sergei Batovrin has reported that early in 1983 at the Sverdlovsk Transfer Prison Shatravka was discovered by guards to have addressed a letter to Western peace activists: he was taken into the prison yard, stripped, and beaten with clubs and rubber hoses. He has subsequently suffered severe illness, been on hunger strike, and, in the summer of 1984, exhausted by repeated beatings, attempted to take his own life. It was after hearing such reports that Bruce Kent held a vigil, in August 1984, on behalf of Shatravka and also Dr Dikerdem, President of the Turkish Peace Association.+

---

* The Appeal called upon the general public of the USA and USSR 'to create integrated, international public groups based on the principles of independence, whose functions would be to accept and analyze individual proposals for disarmament and the establishment of trust between countries'.

† The Appeal had called for the governments of the USA and USSR to create an international bulletin in which both sides entered into open dialogue, and which carried information on disarmament negotiations, and 'an exchange of information about the possible consequences of using nuclear weaponry'.

\+ There is good news for once (November 1984). Dr Dikerdem has been released from prison, although several of his colleagues in the

It will be seen that this Commission reached much the same conclusion as our own learned Lord Chief Justice Lane, that 'national security' is whatever the government says it is, and that all citizens must defer to this 'constitutional norm'. But the Soviet authorities, especially in distant Tyumen, have a great many more teeth than our own authorities are yet provided with; and they use them. If Lord Chief Justice Lane and Mrs Thatcher or President Reagan, sometimes drive some of us into dissident mentalities, then how much more bitter must be the dissident mentality of Soviet citizens who have bumped against rabid ideology masked as law. Before Western peace activists start calling such reactions 'anti-Soviet' they should reflect that Batovrin and Shatravka are 'Soviet' also, just as both Tolstoy and Lenin are part of the Russian inheritance; and that if they had been confined to psychiatric institutes or beaten up with rubber hoses for their peace activities, then they might now be more 'anti-British' or 'anti-American' than they are.

If some potential friends in Communist states have been driven into dissident mentalities, the credit should be given to the KGB which intends to drive them there. It wishes to isolate and alienate critics from that large sector of middle opinion which recalls the horrors of World War II, which justly finds Western militarism menacing, which has no taste for any actions which would lead them into a life of harassment and yet which yearns for democratic changes and a human opening to the West. The dissident mentality, while fully understandable and indeed inevitable, cannot offer any strategy for healing the Cold War so long as it is a simple inversion of 'only-two-sides'—a sort of flip-over from one 'side' to the other. (Such flip-overs happen sometimes in the West as in the East). The Moscow Trust Group has had the temptation of this inversion pressed upon it again and again, and the record of harassment in Sergei Batovrin's *Return*

Turkish Peace Association remain in prison awaiting a fresh trial. Also recent accounts suggest that Alexander Shatravka's treatment in his prison-camp has much improved in the past few months. In both cases publicity and the representations of the peace movement appear to have had some effect.

Address: Moscow makes painful reading; yet what is most remarkable is the way in which the group has risen above its persecution again and again, and has continued, with restraint, to search for a third way.

I do not know if the Trust Group will succeed in its courageous project. In the most optimistic view it may have opened the door a crack, through which an increasing informal traffic of trust will flow, until the Party's taboo upon unlicensed citizen exchanges with Western peace activists has to give way. At that stage one would expect that much more widespread informal channels for international exchanges would come into being, which would manage to disengage from confrontations with the authorities. But for this to take place, the authorities also would have to modify their sacred rule (the 'leading role of the Party'), and the Soviet Peace Committee itself would have to learn to tolerate peaceful co-existence within the USSR with other kinds of citizen peace initiatives.

IV 'DECAYING IDEOLOGICAL RUBBISH'

I must now return from a long digression. I was explaining why Soviet ideologists commenced to lampoon END and substantial sections of the Western peace movement, and why Yuri Zhukov, of the Soviet Peace Committee, sent out his divisive letter in December 1982. This led me to our relations with independent peace groups in the East, and I have tried to explain their complexity by sketching two examples: Hungary, where there has been a little space for independence, and the USSR, where there has been no space at all. The cases of the GDR, Czechoslovakia and Poland would reveal equal complexities. From the first moment of martial law in Poland it was apparent that our strategy of resisting Western nuclear arms while at the same time seeking for human openings to the East would encounter heavy resistance. By the winter of 1982–3 this evidence was accumulating: the harassment of 'Swords into Ploughshares' in the GDR, the arrest of Ladislav Lis of Charter 77, the unceasing pressure on the Trust Group, and a Warsaw Pact summit (January 5, 1983) which combined a series of disarmament proposals addressed to Western opinion with more private discussions on re-establishing the 'leading role of the Party'. It was in these circumstances that I published, in late February 1983, my article on the 'Soviet "Peace Offensive" ' in the *Guardian* and the *Nation*.

It was not well liked. It made some people angry in both the British and American peace movements. The British movement, especially CND, was flexing its muscles in the year which was expected to 'refuse cruise'. The American movement was resisting MX and the B-1 and was getting ready to help with Pershing II and cruise. Both were standing up against a growing torrent of anti-Communist invective, and were seeking to discount the aggressive enemy image that was being projected (by aggressive ideologists) upon the Soviet Union. The disarmament proposals of the Warsaw Pact summit (several of which were good) had been welcomed. And in any case, what could possibly be wrong with a Soviet 'peace offensive'?

Very possibly I pitched my article in the wrong tone. I commenced by warning the Western peace movement that it was 'sleepwalking into a situation of extraordinary complexity'. This caused offence; no-one could accept that *they* had been sleepwalking. And yet I think that we all had nodded off on our marching feet once or twice. We had not noticed the shift in the terms of political argument in the previous year which had come with Reagan's 'zero option'. In terms of 'balance' and 'arms control' Reagan's proposal was clearly specious: in offering that the Russians should take out, not only all their SS-20s but all their SS-4s and SS-5s, he was generously offering that the Soviet Union should reduce its European nuclear arsenal to the level of 1960 while not one reduction was made on NATO's side. It is now generally acknowledged that the 'zero option'—

> Could not provide the basis for serious negotiation and was not meant to do so. It was a position constructed purely for show, one designed to make the administration look generous in offering to give up any deployment of missiles, while at the same time assuring that the negotiations got nowhere.
>
> (George W. Ball, *NY Review of Books*, November 8, 1984.)

This is to say that the 'zero option' was intended not to disarm any nuclear weapons but to disarm the Western peace movement. Sensing that this was so, the peace movement confronted the 'zero option' with ridicule and refusal; and in doing so, it fell, not into a Soviet, but into a Reagan trap. In 1980 and 1981 the swelling movement had united behind the positive demand: for a nuclear-free Europe! After the 'zero option', in 1982 and 1983, the argument had been subtly tipped, so that the peace movement appeared to be arguing on the side of the Soviet negotiating position—that is in favour of the retention of *x* number of SS-20s. But a non-aligned movement ought not to have allowed itself to have been manoeuvred into the position of seeming to defend any nuclear weapons whatsoever.

Was there an alternative? Reagan's public relations staff did not intend us to find one. Within ten minutes of Reagan's 'zero option' speech I was rung on transatlantic phone to demand my instant reactions. So was Bruce Kent, and so, no doubt, were a score of 'spokespersons' of the European peace movement. We were supposed, instantly, to say 'yes' or 'no'. If 'yes', then that was a victory for Reagan; if 'no', then we were exposed as pro-Soviet which was another victory for Reagan. With our slender resources no instant conference of European movements was possible. In the next few days I was with Daniel Ellsberg in West Germany. Ellsberg was convinced that the hawks in the Pentagon were shaking on their talons, for fear that the Soviet Union might go a long way to *accept* the 'zero option'. He suggested that the peace movement should say 'yes' if (but only if) the 'zero option' was combined with an across-the-board nuclear weapons freeze. I suggested a different response: we should say 'yes, but more', and demand that more be thrown in on the Western side—for example, Polaris and Pershing IA—as a sweetener. (Bruce Kent suggested much the same in a letter to the *Guardian.*) The West German peace movement leaders (including Greens) were not even interested in sitting down at a table with our British and American delegation and discussing it. The Krefeld Appeal had never mentioned SS-20s. The West German movement at that time was reluctant to direct any criticism at Soviet militarism, in part through the understandable historical legacy of guilt for World War II and the vast Soviet losses of that war. When Ellsberg and I raised the issue at a meeting in West Berlin our reception was stormy. Reagan's offer was a 'trick' (it was), and in the German view it should be confronted and 'exposed', whereas in our view it should be trumped by an even more far-reaching demand.

I suppose that the outcome was inevitable. Mass protest movements cannot engage in subtle diplomacy. They are 'yes' and 'no' movements, and the more nuanced proposals of Ellsberg, Bruce Kent or myself—given fleeting media exposure or none at all—could not become visible within the high-visibility shouting-match on every media channel of the opposed superpowers and their allies.

The ensuing Geneva 'negotiations' which dragged through 1982 and 1983 were negotiations not to control arms but to control public opinion. Reagan and Caspar Weinberger, and their conspiratorial advisers, Richard Perle and Richard Burt—as is documented abundantly in Strobe Talbott's *Deadly Gambits*—never desired the negotiations to reach a resolution, were determined to put down the new missiles in Europe, and were (and still are) reaching for clear nuclear superiority in every field (whatever that may mean). As the *Wall Street Journal* remarked candidly (October 7th, 1983) United States postures of negotiating 'flexibility' were—

> Perhaps the most important element of a multifaceted West European strategy aimed at countering peace movements and getting ready for the likely deployment of 572 US medium-range missiles.

As for the Soviet Union, in 1982 and the first months of 1983 it was also playing to Western public opinion, hoping to pick apart NATO 'modernisation' (and also perhaps NATO) with the help of peace movements and the German and British elections. Only in the last months of 1983, when Andropov was dying, did it come up with hard and, in arms control terms, acceptable proposals. At that stage Mrs Thatcher and Mr Heseltine helped on their American backers by putting the boot in; they rushed in the first flight of cruise missiles to Greenham Common, a month in advance of the date announced by NATO, in order to foreclose any further negotiations or public discussion. It had been throughout a negotiation between two con-men with public opinion as the patsy.

In these circumstances it was necessary and honourable in the Western peace movement to expose the spoof of the 'zero option'. And any peace movement deserving the name had to assert its unconditional and implacable refusal of cruise and Pershing II. (The well-intentioned 'multilateralists' were being conned even more dishonestly than were the 'unilateralists'.) Yet mere opposition, without a large and imaginative transcontinental alternative, of necessity appeared to cast the peace movement in the role of auxiliary to Soviet negotiators—a casting which Western media and politicians did all in their power to enforce. This perception was also transmitted to a wide public in Eastern Europe, where an unholy alliance of Communist media and Western 'free radio' operations projected the Western movement as pro-Soviet and one-sided, and suppressed all mention of the reciprocal demands made on the Warsaw powers.

That is why I wrote 'The Soviet "Peace Offensive" ' in February 1983. It seemed to me at that time that it was more necessary than ever, if we were to hold onto middle opinion in Europe and America, that we should enforce our non-aligned perspective, repudiate the role of auxiliary to either side, and even attempt to extract concessions (whether cuts in SS-20s or more fluent citizen exchanges with the East) from the Soviet Union. If we could not do this then I foresaw defeat; and it gives me no satisfaction that this defeat (with the return to power of Kohl and Thatcher) took place as I foretold.

What happened in 1983–4 was that the ideological confrontation *between* the blocs was displaced, in an extraordinary way, by an internal ideological civil war *within* each bloc. Thus in Britain the traditional Right fought it out, not with the Russians, but with CND, the Greenham Women and with the traditional domestic Left (the Labour Party). In the Warsaw bloc the Communist hard-liners re-established their disciplinary rule over Solidarnosc, Charter 77, all 'dissidents', and over their own Party. And, in a final episode, the Republicans in the United States in November 1984 wreaked their vengeance in a Massacre of the Democratic Innocents. The extent of the defeat of 1983-4 is expressed, not only in the nuclear excreta strewn on the territory of Europe, East and West, and increasingly washing around in the Atlantic, Pacific, Mediterranean and Indian oceans, but also in the fact that in the twin succession-crises in both superpowers the armourers and ideologists pushed their own hard-liner to the top. The hawks had fed the Other's hawks.

The argument of which this article was a part has trickled on ever since. It arose simultaneously in many places and languages; from Holland (Mient-Jan Faber and the Dutch IKV), from both Germanies (notably the Greens), from Britain (Mary Kaldor and others in *END Journal*), from France, Italy and the United States, but also—commencing from different perceptions—from Eastern Europe and the Soviet Union. The growing confluence of East/West public opinion, the 'peace-and-freedom' mood of 1981-2, was reversed in 1983-4 as the blocs hardened against each other. It seemed to some, as it had seemed in the first cold war, that one must either be for a (pro-Soviet) 'peace' or for a (pro-Western) 'freedom': one could not be for a non-aligned *both*. In the Western peace movement some viewed the issue as a distracting debate about 'human rights'; and I debated it in these terms in the *Nation* ('The Wisdom of Solomon', in *The Heavy Dancers*). Yet I regard this debate as itself a diversion. Human rights are being violated in every part of the globe. But if we consider the problems of peace-making, not only with respect to the instruments and symbols of bloc confrontation (nuclear weapons), but in a full political and cultural perspective, then it becomes obvious that any healing of the blocs entails greater rights of citizen communication and expression, not as a precondition to disarmament ('linkage') nor as a wished-for consequence of disarmament, but as an integral part of the process of making peace.

The political problem is neither armaments (alone) nor human rights (alone) but the very condition out of which confrontations, new weapons-systems, and the repression of rights continually arise. This condition is the bloc-division of the world itself, and specifically the division of Europe, and it is this which we must address if civilization is to survive. It is of the first importance that voices have been answering us from the East in similar terms. The most significant have come from Central Europe where, in Czechoslovakia, the GDR and Hungary, there are cultural resources derived from both the Communist and the Western democratic traditions. It was the Czechoslovak civil rights organisation, Charter 77, which (at risk to itself) initiated a long and searching dialogue with the Western peace movement; and the most luminous essay on the whole problem of making 'a democratic peace' has come from Dr Jaroslav Šabata, a veteran first of the Communist Party (until 1968) and then of the human rights movement (for which he has suffered years of imprisonment), now in retirement at Brno. (See *Voices from Prague*, Palach Press/END, 1983.) It is a discussion which continues.

Official ideologists of the Communist bloc have not tried to join the discourse but to close it down altogether, either by police measures or by political hard-porn. Shortly before the World Peace Council's 'Assembly for Peace and Life' in Prague in June 1983 (which itself was organised as a reply to the non-aligned European Nuclear Disarmament Convention in Berlin the month before), a private Czech Communist Party security briefing for its activists was disclosed (perhaps by a cousin of Sarah Tisdall in Prague?). This noted that 'imperialism' was trying to weaken the peace movement 'by infiltrating it with ideas, persons and whole organisations whose clear aim is to break the peace movement, to prevent its unification, etc.' These wicked groups 'are apparently conducted and financed directly from the centre of CIA and similar agencies', and END was the first of such organisations listed ('with explicit anti-Communist and anti-Soviet function'), whose 'best-known personality is Professor Thompson', along with 'numerous exiles from socialist countries'. I have already noted examples of this porn which is now being manufactured by the metre, and which is too repetitious to merit further attention.

It is curious that argument has not been joined, since the ideologists on the other side could mount a plausible case against our strategy of a 'thaw' or 'healing-process' between the citizenry of the blocs. They could mount *two* cases: a (thin) public case, and a private, or *sotto voce*, case which is stronger. It has been left to an American polemicist, Professor Mark Solomon,* to argue the public case, in a polemic, *Death Waltz to Armageddon: E.P. Thompson and the Peace Movement*, which has been dutifully extracted and translated, in several languages, in the organ-of-export of the Soviet Peace Committee, *Twentieth Century and Peace*.

Mark Solomon is a zealous pro-Soviet only-two-sidesman, and an example of that process of 'inversion' or dissident mentality which I have already discussed. He does not write badly, and the best way of describing his *Death Waltz* is to say that it is like a tract in which the right-hand page only is printed and the left-hand is left blank. On the right-hand page we have a record of the sins of successive United States governments in driving forward the nuclear arms race; much of this is true, it is relevant, and it should be remembered. On the left-hand page (where we might expect some corresponding record of Soviet behaviour) there is nothing: a sweet blank: no discussion of Soviet conventional armaments, of the division of Europe, of the occupation of Czechoslovakia by Warsaw Pact forces in 1968, a dismissive reference to my 'reflexive' views on Afghanistan. Where the Soviet Union does appear is on the right-hand page, as ecstatic points of light to throw into even deeper shadow the murky acts and intentions of the USA. Solomon's mythic descriptions of Soviet society ('the absence of a basic antagonism between government and public', 'consistent, mutually supportive relationship between the majority of the Soviet public and the government's diplomatic and defense policies') and of the 'independence' of the Soviet Peace Committee with its '130 million' members would be hilarious if it were not that the realities are so sad and anxious.

* I am told that Mark Solomon, who is an officer of the small U.S. Peace Council (affiliated to the World Peace Council), is not to be confused with Norman Solomon. It seems that 'Solomon' is a sobriquet (like 'General Ludd', etc.) which is employed by pro-Soviet polemicists in the United States to signal their surpassing wisdom.

I will take one sample of Mark Solomon's polemic:

> Thompson regularly ignites the combustible materials that inflame the Cold War. He has stated, for example, that the Soviet Union is untrustworthy because 'the information available to its citizens is strictly controlled and. . . public opinion can scarcely influence the rulers'. But Thompson does not indicate what information is withheld from Soviet citizens. Widely distributed literature on the nature of nuclear war, publicized television programs featuring US and Soviet physicians discussing the medical effects of a nuclear holocaust, the public contributions of Soviet scientists on 'nuclear winter', even graveyard humour about nuclear war, are all known aspects of Soviet life.

Unlike Professor Solomon I am not an authority on the Soviet media and information services. But I have discussed these matters with authorities (and with Soviet citizens) and have been given different accounts. I have been told that there is, indeed, a great deal of daily information (or propaganda) about nuclear weapons. But 95% of this is about *Western* nuclear weapons, and the aggressive designs of imperialism; and perhaps 5% gives reassurance that the Soviet military are also preparing those weapons which are essential for the Soviet people's 'defence'. This is to say that the information available to the Soviet public might be fairly compared with that available to the British public if they had been reduced, in 1983, to abject dependency on such brochures as the Ministry of Defence prepared under the strong guidance of Mr Heseltine—comprised of charts of SS-20s and the Soviet military build-up, together with a recommendation of cruise missiles as an 'insurance policy' for peace.

There is, in addition, much media coverage of manifestations by the Western peace movement, Greenham Common and so forth. What is absent is (a) any hard information about Soviet weaponry, etc. (Even the code-names for Soviet missiles are those used by Western intelligence, as are the estimates of their numbers.) (b) Any publication of any Western peace movement programmes and policies, appeals or books, which contain any whisper of criticism of any

Soviet military or ideological posture. (c) Objective scientific works on nuclear questions are not available, unless in certain restricted specialist libraries—even the SIPRI (Stockholm Peace Research) annual handbook must be taken in by Western visitors—and may be impounded at customs. (d) As a matter of course, publications which raise questions critical of Soviet military and diplomatic policies are disallowed, so that if it is true (as Professor Solomon insists) that the Soviet public support all their government's policies, this might perhaps be because they are not permitted to read about or discuss any others.

During 1983 some scientists associated with the Moscow Trust Group, who had been influenced by the pioneering work in peace research of the British Quaker mathematician, Professor L.F. Richardson, commenced econometric researches and attempted to elaborate an index of international tension by measuring the centimetres in the press devoted to hostile commentary on the Other. I do not know whether this is a valid approach or not. In any event, in the aftermath of the shooting-down of the Korean airliner, KAL 007, Professor Yuri Medvedkov wrote to me in the greatest alarm. Their index had suddenly sky-rocketed through the roof.

Yuri Medvedkov added: 'The most horrible rhetoric each day can be heard over the TV or radio. . . The man in the street gets lots of hatred propaganda.' He added that as a result he expected the Geneva talks to fail, and the efforts to secure a freeze would be indefinitely delayed. The Soviet public were filled with fears that there were 'plans in the West to start any night a preventive nuclear strike against Russia'. He urged upon Western peace activists every possible measure 'to keep channels open for constant dialogue'.

A count of the column inches of anti-Soviet material in the New York or London *Times* in that period would be equally alarming. It will be recalled that President Reagan used the incident to shoot down, not the Russians, but the US peace movement, forcing through a shattered Congress budgetary appropriations for the MX missile and for binary nerve-gas facilities. Whether centralised and censored or private and 'free' the major media did their own sensational thing on both sides and piled tension upon tension.

But we have strayed from the main point, which is Professor Solomon's confidence that the Soviet public is well-informed on all nuclear and international matters, that it has studied these matters with care and on every issue has freely decided to support government policies, and that, unlike us anarchistic Westerners, it stands in no need of any independent organisations or any area of uncontrolled press which might offer alternative information or even criticism of Soviet military and diplomatic policies in Soviet public life simply because (unless in the minds of a handful of embittered 'dissidents') there are no criticisms which an open-minded Soviet citizen could possibly sustain.

As it happens I have in front of me an 'Open Letter' to Professor Solomon which discusses these points in passing. It is written by Dr Mark Reitman, a member of the Moscow Trust Group, who is a mathematician, now invalided from work as a result of Parkinson's disease and diabetes. Dr Reitman writes that the fact that the information available to Soviet citizens is strictly controlled 'is not challenged by the Soviet government. . . and we are, unfortunately, obliged to confirm it':

> You say that television broadcasts in which Soviet and American physicians discussed the medical consequences of nuclear catastrophe were widely publicised in the USSR. True, these broadcasts were widely publicised, especially in the West. But why do you refer to them in the plural? Such a programme occurred only once, although its participants announced that it would become a regular feature. Evidently some powerful forces interfered with this. . .
>
> A citizen of the USSR, even if he were highly committed to the cause of peace, would find it difficult to obtain detailed and balanced information other than from the mouth of Yuri Zhukov. In particular, information about the possible calamities to come, about all aspects of a nuclear death, about the 'nuclear winter', about 'conversion': a simple survey or opinion-poll of the Muscovite intelligentsia shows that they know virtually nothing about it—in fact I myself quite recently confused 'the nuclear winter' with 'the freeze'!

I do not make this argument because I view the situation to be hopeless. On the contrary, the higher regions of Soviet administration may now be occupied by tensions between the old hard forces of control and forces looking for 'modernisation' or even democratic openings. There has been one good TV discussion between Soviet and American physicians, and with pressure from the Soviet public and the Western peace movement there might well be more. There has been one Scandinavian Women's Peacemarch through Soviet cities, and with pressure such manifestations by Western peace activists might be permitted more often. With determined pressure we might even see some centimetres of *Izvestia*'s columns given over to faithful reporting of the policies of non-aligned Western movements. What I wish to do is to rubbish the sentimental mythology promoted by Mark Solomon and others, which is damaging and counter-productive. So long as Western peace workers doze over Noddy books like his, they will be helplessly unprepared to meet events, and they will not press steadily, with self-respect and without provocation, for the human openings essential for the making of peace.*

There is in fact a more plausible case to be found within Solomon's polemic, and it is one which appeals to Western peace workers who honourably desire to redress the anti-Soviet rhetoric of their own societies by coming to a better understanding of Soviet perceptions. This case has three leading propositions.

First, it is asserted that at every stage the United States has led in the nuclear arms race, and that the Soviet Union has been in an 'arms chase' from behind, reacting defensively to Western initiatives. Therefore it follows that the onus is upon the United States, or NATO, to be the first to stop. And the Soviet Union will then follow, to a halt or a freeze.

This is a strong and significant argument. The United States has an atrocious record as pace-setter in nuclear

* A companion volume to Mark Solomon's *Death Waltz to Armageddon* has now been published in Britain: this is Professor V.L. Allen's *Images and Reality in the Soviet Union: or Professor Noddy's Trip to Utopia.*

weaponry, and the record of France and Britain is little better. Caspar Weinberger and his advisers are now clearly going for across-the-board superiority. Inevitably this nourishes fears among their Soviet analogues of Western nuclear blackmail or a decapitating strike. The Western peace movement is right to call 'stop!', and if need be unilaterally. The nuclear arms race has long been in part about 'face'. In Wilfred Owen's parable of the Old Man and the Young, Abram prepares Isaac for sacrifice when an angel appears and offers the Ram of Pride as substitute—

> But the old man would not so, but slew his son,
> And half the seed of Europe, one by one.

If the nuclear arms race cannot be stopped without the sacrifice of the Ram of Pride by one side or the other, then it is in the West, where the pace has usually been set and where public opinion can be brought to bear upon power, that the sacrifice must first be made.

It is also probably true that the Soviet government is now, and has been for several years, more anxious to put a cork on the nuclear arms race than the Americans. It has no taste to follow the United States into scenarios of space wars; it knows very well that in most areas the United States has the technological edge on the Soviet Union; and the diversion of skills and resources to armaments inflicts great damage on the Soviet economy and society. As a Soviet colonel has said, in an off-the-record interview:

> We do have internal problems: we need an economic reform, we need to expand human rights in our country and further to develop Soviet democracy. And we can only make headway in tackling our problems under conditions of prolonged detente. We need detente, lots and lots of detente.
>
> (*Detente*, October 1984.)

This is not to say that there are no Soviet hawks (whom Western hawks are doing their best to strengthen), nor that Soviet negotiators will not be as hard-nosed as those of the United States. It is to say that the main thrust of the nuclear arms race is now from the USA (with Britain), and that Soviet professions of a desire for a freeze and for extensive measures of arms control are a good deal less spurious than professions of Western leaders.

This argument is good. But it has limits. It narrows the question down to that of nuclear weapons only. It is silent about conventional weapons; it is silent about the political and ideological components of bloc confrontation; and it confuses historical origins with present consequences. (Such writers as the two Solomons are strangely silent as to the means by which the USSR made the prodigious stretch forward to nuclear 'parity', and as to the consequences of this assertion of 'balance'). The argument has been presented most ably by Roy and Zhores Medvedev, and I have criticised its limitations in 'Exterminism Reviewed'

Second, we are enjoined—in the pursuit of peace—to set aside all considerations which do not bear directly upon nuclear weapons and their control. It is said that an 'anti-war movement' must narrow its focus, not to the occasions of war and the causes of tension, but to the nuclear instruments only, and that any other matter is extraneous and divisive. This is a bad argument. It offers to disinfect our cruel historical experience of all political and ideological content. It can drag the peace movement into the tit-for-tat rituals of 'balance'. At worst, it leaves us like the spectators at Wimbledon, craning our necks as the ball goes to and fro between the superpowers, cheering on one side. Much of my writing in the past three years presents a counter-argument, and I will leave it at that.

Third, we are enjoined to recall the Soviet people's prodigious losses in World War II (and, indeed, in the earlier wars of intervention) and to understand their deeply defensive mentality. This is also a good and significant argument. But its significance must be examined with some care.

The figure which is customarily used to indicate Soviet losses in World War II is some twenty million lives. This is approximate only, and to this must be added the wholesale destruction of towns and villages, of industrial and agricultural plant, of schools, of livestock, and the 'scorched earth' of the western and southern regions (including the most productive and populous regions) of the Soviet Union. It is as if the whole of New England, New York State and some of the Mid-West of the USA, together with a large part of its population, had been 'taken out'. There is no way in which such an experience will not have traumatised the Soviet historical memory.

Critics of Soviet policies sometimes offer qualifications, but certain of these are beside the point. It is true that other European nations suffered comparable *pro rata* losses (for example, Poland and Yugoslavia). But this does not lessen Soviet losses by one digit; at the most it suggests that the Soviet memory of the 'Great Patriotic War' is selective and ungenerous to the losses of others, as is the way of all nations. (Americans, whose folk-and-media memory of World War II is absurdly US-centric, should be the last to complain.) It is also true that umpteen million lives were lost in the previous two decades by the self-inflicted savagery of Stalinist purges, the liquidation of the kulaks, and so on. But this also is beside the point. These losses have inflicted their own traumas, but the healing of those wounds (if they can be healed) is a matter which the Soviet people must resolve amongst themselves. Whereas the losses inflicted by Hitler's armies are remembered as an unprovoked act of aggression, delivered without warning, and inflicted from 'the West'. This laid down a ground in Soviet popular expectation which is easily stirred into anxiety: may there not be 'plans in the West to start any night a preventive nuclear strike against Russia'?

It is necessary to bear these perceptions in mind also when considering the difficult questions of 'Yalta' and the division of Europe. I argue repeatedly in *The Heavy Dancers* that these are proper and central questions for the peace movement, and that we must place them on the agenda. But this cannot be done in a way which offends against what is just in Soviet historical experience. Glib cold warriors today imply that the entry of Soviet armies into Central and Eastern Europe in 1944-5 was done with premeditated and aggressive intent, which 'Yalta' then condoned. But this is not how men and women of my own generation remember the event. We recall a Europe totally subordinated to Nazi and Fascist militarism; and then Soviet armies (fighting sometimes, as in the suburbs of Stalingrad, with petrol-bottles and their bare hands) forcing that invincible and implacable military machine backwards, long before the Western Allies had launched their long-trumpeted Second Front. Soviet armies entered Central Europe and advanced to the Elbe in pursuit of Hitler's armies, and they were at that stage no more engaged in actions of expansion than were the armies of the Western Allies in Italy, Holland or France. If Soviet armies remained in East Germany, so also do American, British and French armies remain in West Germany to this day. And it was the Western Allies who tore up their treaty obligations by initiating West German rearmament.

I apologise for rehearsing this brutal historical ABC, but I find that in some discussions of 'Yalta' it is forgotten, even by sections of the peace movement. The historical origins of the division of Europe condone nothing that followed; and (in the East) they do not condone the betrayal of Poland, the twice-repeated betrayal of Czechoslovak democracy, and the Stalinist rigours throughout the whole region. These are the traumas which we now have to heal. But we cannot heal them if we offend the historical memory of the Soviet public, if we suppress the record of Soviet suffering and valour, and view 'Yalta' only from the Western side.*

* A brochure prepared by 'Solidarity' (the Solidarność Information Office in London) refers to 'the infamous Yalta Conference which resulted in the enslavement of more than 150 million people in Central and Eastern Europe [and which] made the Soviet Union the greatest threat to world peace since the demise of Hitler's Third Reich'. It calls on the British government to 'renounce Yalta', advertising a public meeting in support of this demand (February 4th, 1985) to be addressed by Winston Churchill, M.P. President Reagan, during his election campaign, gratified a section of his Polish-American constituents with a similar rhetorical repudiation of 'Yalta', while Zbigniew Brzezinski has called in the *New York Times* for a 'well-funded French-British-West German-Italian consortium to aid Eastern European efforts to emancipate peacefully', in supplement to American aid in support of dissident 'subversion'. Such bald incitements, which revive the rhetoric of John

The Soviet popular memory of the losses of war is just and to be respected. Yet we still have to enquire whether this is an influence which, in every circumstance, is making for peace. And the evidence here is contradictory. It does not necessarily follow that great suffering disposes a nation to peace: there are historical examples on the other side. We may take it that, in the Soviet case, it has enforced a desire for peace. Yet this finds expression in a willingness to concede to the Soviet rulers extraordinary authority over every matter concerned with Soviet 'defence', to ensure that the experience of 1941–44 shall never be repeated. In the name of 'defence' the Soviet public has seemed to be willing to accept the diversion of vast resources to military expenditure, restrictions upon civil rights, and restraints upon living standards. It is precisely in their highly-advertised role as defenders of 'peace' against Western (or Chinese) imperialist aggression that the old-guard post-Stalinist leadership legitimises its rule and resists long-overdue reforms.

We have, then, a paradox: the Soviet public has a peaceful disposition, and Western visitors to the USSR are overwhelmed with peaceful assurances which are heartfelt and sincere. Yet the USSR is a society in which the visibility of the military is higher than in any Western democracy. Great events of state, parades in Red Square, solemn state funerals, have the highest military symbolism. They signal that this is a nation which feels itself to be threatened and besieged in which the prime function of the rulers is to build up the nation's defences, and in which all else must be subordinated to these priorities.

The traumas of World War II also left numb the Soviet internationalist conscience. In popular memory the USSR is seen as the victim of external invasion, and the memory imposes itself on the perception of the present. I am told that the ordinary man or woman in a Moscow queue concern themselves little about the policies of their rulers towards

Foster Dulles, do nothing to advance the causes of civil rights or of Polish autonomy, destroy the chances of a healing-process between the blocs, and should be repudiated by independent peace forces in West or East. We can never permit the ideologists and agencies of the cold war to set our own citizens agenda.

Czechoslovakia or Afghanistan; if they grumble, it may be about supporting lazy and ungrateful Poles, or subsidising indigent Third World nations at the expense of their own standard of living. They do, however, believe in the reality of the threat of the Other, just as the majority of the British and American public have proved themselves to be true believers; and, like our own publics, they endorse 'defence'.

I became, a year or two ago, a little vexed by the Simple Solomons who repeatedly assure us that, because the Soviet people suffered grievously forty years ago, their rulers could not possibly, in any circumstances, take an unpeaceful action today. And I wrote, inadvisedly, in February 1983 about Soviet 'paranoia', and added:

> Those weeping Soviet grandmothers who still deck with flowers the graves of the last war have dry eyes for Afghanistan, as they had, in 1968, for Czechoslovakia. The Soviet people will support their rulers in preparations for any war that is 'in defence of peace'.

No sentences which I have written gave more offence to some in the peace movement. And I am convinced that they truly offended some Soviet readers, not only in form but in reality. A year later, at a conference in Athens, Mr Yuri Zhukov quoted these lines and proclaimed them to be an insult to the entire Soviet people which unmasked my pretences to be any kind of advocate of peace. Mr Zhukov is a great showman, who has a regular slot on prime-time Soviet TV in which he 'answers' letters about war and peace, but on this occasion I think he spoke from his heart. My words seemed to him, when set against the remembered suffering of World War II, to be obscene.

I have been asked: why did I write these lines? I did not write them to mock the grief of Soviet grandmothers, and if it seems otherwise then the words were ill-written. I was vexed with the Soviet apologists (especially in the West) who increasingly invoked these grandmothers in order to deflect us into sentiment and away from any analysis of Soviet policies. There are, after all, some grandmothers and grandfathers in the West, who still cherish graves of the last war, but who do not for that reason remain silent about their own governments' sins. I wrote those lines simply because I think that they are true. The Soviet public, like great sections of the Western public, will support all military preparations in the name of 'defence'; and perhaps will support them even more readily because of its historical memories of the horrors of war. A war 'in defence of peace' has been going on now for five years in Afghanistan, and the Soviet public (which may approve of it less than it did) has not yet been able to find any means to call its course in question.

Yet the argument which enforces Soviet war experiences remains a sound and important argument. Undoubtedly the Soviet people are of a peaceful disposition; the very notion of war fills them with nausea; and this may be contrasted with the disposition of a section of the American public which, never having suffered such experiences on American territory, can be whipped up into shallow and braggart clamour to 'stand up to the Commies' everywhere, so long as this can be done by space-age technological marvels and on some other nation's territory and without risk to one drop of sacred American blood. If the Soviet public is encouraged to perpetuate World War II memories with familial rituals—for example, the newly-weds visiting the graves of their kin on their wedding-day—then this may cement Soviet patriotism but it is not a source of braggart adventurism. Such ceremonial pieties merit Western respect, and not least from that other part of the American public which is seeking to understand this combination of Soviet defensiveness and pride.

But the peaceful disposition of a people who have no means to inform themselves on military questions, and who cannot voice criticisms nor discuss alternative policies, does not take us very far. It has taken a good number of Soviet citizens, in 1983 and 1984, into a number of actions and demonstrations organised on their behalf by the Soviet Peace Committee, in response to the Western peace movement. On these occasions the slogans are usually determined (and the placards are manufactured) by the organisers, and it is satisfactory to note that more even-handed slogans have now appeared than the old denunciations of Western imperialism. In particular the slogan has now appeared: 'No Nuclear Weapons in Europe, West or East! No nuclear weapons anywhere in the world!' I take this to be an advance, even though no slogans critical of Soviet weaponry are permitted, and the speeches and demands continue to be directed against the West.

I have no doubt that many of the demonstrators in Moscow and other cities genuinely wished to further the cause of peace. There is some kind of stirring in public opinion going on. In the summer of 1984 some members of the Moscow Trust Group sallied out into Moscow streets with an unauthorised petition calling on the leaders of the USSR and USA to hold a summit meeting. They also met with a ready response, from a random selection of the public who knew that the petition was not 'official'. Dr Mark Reitman, who shares the view of myself (and Mark Solomon) that the Soviet people are disposed to peace, described the incident in his 'Open Letter':

> We saw how unanimously Soviet people spoke out on behalf of peace when we gathered signatures. . . We saw close up the faces of women, stooping heavily under the load of their shopping bags when they read the short text of the appeal and signed it, not without difficulty freeing the right hand from its burden. These were impressive faces. Like the faces of three men from a kvas queue, who at first stood indifferent and motionless, but who hastily added their signatures onto the disappearing sheet when the militia and the police dragged one of us off into a car. These are the people Thompson refers to as 'the third force'.
>
> You, comrade Solomon, are enraptured by 'columns of quietly determined marchers carrying signs demanding that weapons of mass destruction be banished everywhere'. But I would venture to point out that marching under banners and slogans is not very difficult when you have been specially released from work or lectures for this purpose, and the boss has instructed you as to which column you are to join. Far more striking is the determination to stand up for peace under extraordinary conditions. . .

We are all agreed, then—myself, Dr Reitman, and the Venerable Solomon—that the Soviet people want peace. This strengthens the case of the Western peace movement. We can all agree that this is a time for Western governments, not to pile up new weapons, but to strengthen this peaceful disposition by offering reconciliation and concession. It is also the time (but here Professor Solomon does not agree) for Western peace workers to try to break through the rigid controls set up by the deeply-defensive (and sometimes offensive) security and ideological establishments, and to effect multiple direct contacts with Soviet citizens. This direct communication will also be welcomed by most Soviet citizens, who are yearning for a 'thaw'. In short, our independent friends in East Europe and in Moscow have made the right diagnosis. What we need most of all now is the establishment of trust, and of dialogue, between peoples, without which, whatever the peoples of both sides may 'want', they will not get it. If wishes were horses, beggars would be riders. In a climate of deepening distrust they will get not peace but more weapons and eventually terminal war.

It can be seen that the pro-Soviet only-two-sidesmen have two strong arguments: the United States (with Britain and NATO) are driving forward the nuclear arms race: and there is no evidence that Soviet popular culture nourishes aggressive and expansionist urges. It might seem to follow that this is a moment when the Communist authorities would welcome our strategies for a thaw between peoples and a healing of bloc divisions. Yet some of them have shown themselves to be implacably opposed, to the extent of lampooning non-aligned peace movements as NATO agencies, denying peace activists visas, in certain cases arresting them and throwing them out of their countries, confiscating Western peace materials at the border and intercepting post.

What this suggests is that the public case of pro-Soviet apologists is concealing a private case, which may only be expressed *sotto voce*, if at all. The *sotto voce* case is a strong one, and one which the peace movement should understand and take into account. But by its very nature it is not one which Mr Zhukov or Professor Solomon, or any pro-Soviet apologist, can argue aloud. It is that the Soviet Union after decades of civil war, purges, war and cold war, repression and censorship, finds itself now without any mechanisms of self-reform, and its political and intellectual life has got snarled up into so many knots that the authorities fear any external influences as 'de-stabilising'. If the infection of peace were to pass from West to East, in self-activating forms which exposed the Communist authorities themselves to criticism, then there is no way of estimating into what recesses of Communist society the epidemic might reach.

Mark Solomon could not possibly argue this case, since he has assured his readers that Soviet society is the most stable known to time. There is no antagonism between government and public, and there are 'consistent, mutually supportive' relations between government and public in all matters of defence and foreign policy. That being so, it must puzzle Solomon's readers to know why government takes such careful measures to channel and invigilate relations between Soviet and Western publics, and why a few score of independent-minded peaceniks have been persecuted by the KGB. One would have supposed that if Mark Reitman or Olga Medvedkova had got hold of some mistaken views, then this should be a matter beneath the notice of the state, and it could safely be left to sturdy-minded Soviet citizens to dissuade them or to laugh them out of court. And one would have supposed that if Mient-Jan Faber or Randall Forsberg, Daniel Ellsberg or Mary Kaldor were to hold public lectures and seminars in Leningrad or Moscow, in which they made some even-handed criticisms of both US and Soviet nuclear policies, then it could be left to the good sense of the audience to decide on the merits of the case.

Both suppositions would have been wrong. The Soviet authorities—or at least the old guard among them—are frightened of the least action derogatory to the 'leading role of the Party'. They are fearful of allowing their 'mutually supportive' citizens to stray on their own any further than the end of the Party street. And (at the risk of being called 'anti-Soviet' once again) I will say that I am in turn frightened by a government which places so little trust in its own citizens, and which is one of the world's two great ranchers of nuclear weapons. I cannot see how the peaceful disposition of these citizens can be, in any emergency, an effective restraint upon government.

This is the political bind we are in, and it explains some of the divisions between movements for peace and for 'peace' which have become apparent in 1983 and 1984. So long as it seemed possible that the non-aligned Western movement—German Greens and Social-Democrats, Dutch churches, British CND and Greenham women, American freeze, Italian Eurocommunists—might actually stop cruise and Pershing II deployments, the Soviet ideologists confined themselves to grumbling polemic, slander upon a few individuals, and low-profile attempts at manipulation. Once deployment had taken place, the non-aligned elements (with their suspect independent contacts in the East) became—in orthodox Communist perception—expendable. As Stalin once asked: 'How many divisions has the Pope?' All those untidy myriads of Western marchers had been unable to topple one citadel of Western power. Hard-nosed Communist leaders put the peace movement in a 'pending' file, tried to stub out the sparks of independent groups in the East, and squared up to their real antagonists: Reagan, Thatcher, Kohl. If one takes an only-two-sidesman view, then one can see their point.

But the growing apparatus of Warsaw bloc official peace institutions still had to be found employment. As it seems to me, they were given a new brief. This was to 'unite' the Western and Eastern peace and 'peace' movements behind a common anti-war programme, and, insofar as possible, bring Western movements under the hegemony of the Helsinki-based World Peace Council. In doing so they should be willing to cut their losses. Certain articulate non-aligned spokespersons should be lampooned and driven out (with the help of such materials as those provided by Mark Solomon and Professor V.L. Allen). They should be willing to induce splits in the Western movement, and to tie it up in internecine divisions. The majority Western peace movements were becoming an ill-disciplined nuisance and even making raids into the East. It might now be scattered, and a part of it (even if a minority) should be firmly brought within World Peace Council leadership so that it might still have nuisance-value as auxiliary to Soviet diplomacy.

I take this to have been (and still to be) the brief of the Soviet Peace Committee, which is run by some of the toughest hard-line ideologists in the Warsaw bloc. Its President, Yuri Zhukov, earned his spurs as a *Pravda* columnist (a sort of Soviet Bernard Levin or William Buckley) during the Warsaw Pact 'fraternal' occupation of Czechoslovakia in 1968, and he has recently been sent on a Soviet Party delegation to split the Spanish Communists. To be just, I think the operation has critics among doves even within the Soviet apparatus, and it has never been followed wholeheartedly by the more flexible Hungarian Peace Council.

The operation has not succeeded, although it continues. At Athens in February 1984 there was a conference, hosted by the peace committee of the governing party, PASOK, at which Eastern 'officials' and Western movements met together. I there set out openly the difficulties of comparing like and unlike as if both were 'peace movements'; if Western voluntary organisations, confronting Western militarism, were asked to 'unite' with state-endorsed organisations in the East which were also confronting Western militarism, then we could not regard this as 'a fair swap'. I appealed for a thaw and citizen communication between the blocs ('What Kind of Partnership?' in *The Heavy Dancers*). Professor Hylke Tromp, a leading Dutch peace researcher, Andräs Zumach from West Germany, Chiara Ingrao from Italy, and many others made similar appeals. The conference broke up inconclusively, with some embitterment. In the Soviet hissing that followed, blame was placed upon myself and Mient-Jan Faber (General Secretary of the Dutch IKV), who were alleged, in a Soviet foreign-language hand-out, *News from the USSR*, to have issued exhortations to 'change the socialist system' in the East. In an interview with CND's monthly, *Sanity*, Zhukov used the hospitality of its columns to accuse me of wishing to 'bury the peace movement'.

Throughout the year the weary skirmishing has gone on. In the GDR independent women peace activists, Barbel Bohley and Ulrike Poppe, were arrested after meeting

Barbara Einhorn, an END and CND activist, who was roughly detained, interrogated, and thrown out of the country. Representatives of the IKV and of French CODENE who tried to hold a seminar with members of Charter 77 were thrown out of Czechoslovakia. British, Dutch and West German peace workers have been refused visas to the GDR. Attempts to engage in discussion of the bloc division of Europe, and of means of healing it, have been repudiated indignantly by the Soviet Peace Committee as 'interference in internal affairs' or have been caricatured as 'revanchist, unrealizable dreams of changing the post-war European territorial and political arrangement'. Any attempt to place on the agenda the sensitive 'German question' in any form whatsoever—for example, in Rapacki terms or in terms of the demilitarisation of both Germanies within some loose associative structure—has been denounced without discussion as 'neo-fascist revanchism'. Criticisms by Western peace movements of Soviet missile deployments in Czechoslovakia and the GDR have been repudiated with indignation as products of NATO propaganda. ('The nerves of the Soviet people are strong,' says Zhukov.) The network of campaigning non-aligned Western peace organisations, the IPCC (p. 40), which grew up from its own resources to meet Western needs of consultation and co-ordination is denounced as if it were a trespass upon the World Peace Council's proprietorial cabbage-patch—a Council which lays claim to some superordinate authority over all to do with 'peace'. Yuri Zhukov writes:

> Attempts are being made to isolate the anti-war movements in the West, to place them under a new leadership which would stand in opposition to the World Peace Council.
>
> (*International Life*, June 1984)

After months of painful and time-taking negotiation, delegations from several Warsaw bloc peace committees (including the Soviet) attended at the European Nuclear Disarmament Convention in Perugia. In nearly every case independents from the East were prevented from coming, unless they were already in the West. It was scarcely a dialogue of open minds, and there were discourtesies on both sides which have been sufficiently reported in the peace movements' press. But perhaps dialogue was not what the hard-liners of the Soviet Peace Committee had in mind? Early in October 1984 there was summoned (mostly by give-away air tickets) by the World Peace Council at Helsinki a select private conference of 'Representatives of Peace, Disarmament and Anti-War Movements from Europe and America'. The United States delegation was headed by (surprise!) Professor Mark Solomon, Co-Chair of the US Peace Council. Mr Yuri Zhukov entertained the delegates on the first day with his now-predictable litany of abuse of myself, Mient-Jan Faber, Mary Kaldor and (for novelty) two Finnish Eurocommunists:

> It is not difficult to guess who is interested in forming a bloc of a definite group of organizations acting under the flag of the struggle for peace—a bloc which would abandon the anti-nuclear struggle and devote itself to the struggle aimed at undermining the state system of the socialist countries.

And Zhukov, in the name of 'unity' (!), exerted every effort to drive off the non-aligned movement and to drill the ragged remnants into one united anti-war movement, Peace Councils East and West, behind the demands prescribed by the Bureau of the World Peace Council. According to the TASS report, the conference at Helsinki concluded with a unanimous resolution that:

> The enemies of peace are using extremely subtle methods to undermine the peace movements. Above all they are striving to lead these movements astray from the line of continued struggle against nuclear war and convert them to that other line, the aim of which is a revision of the boundaries formed after the Second World War and intervention in the affairs of the socialist countries. (*Népszabadság*, 9 October 1984).

This kind of attempt at splitting has no chance of success. Anyone who knows anything about the Scandinavian, British,

Dutch, German, Spanish and Italian movements will know this. As for the American movement, its multitudinous amoeboid formations can be split (unless in a few central offices) no more than a knife can split water. But the movements can be confused, diverted into time-wasting ill-tempered arguments, even a little demoralised. In my own view, which is not a majority view, these games of diplomatic footsie between utterly unlike organisations with opposed functions should be brought to an end. We do not have the time or resources for large, inconclusive, snarling conferences. If we wish to attempt dialogue with the 'officials' (which we should) we should opt for smaller and more private fora. If President Reagan is to be serious about arms control he will show it by sacking Richard Perle, and if the Soviet Peace Committee is to be serious about dialogue it will pension off Mr Yuri Zhukov.

The revelation of all this sweet billing and cooing in the dove-cotes of international 'peace' may come as a surprise to some readers, since some of it has been known only to those circles which attend conferences or monitor the Eastern press. Yet it raises issues which should be in the public peace domain. And what the record of the past three years suggests to me is uncertainty. The Communist authorities reveal an extraordinary sense of insecurity in the face of the Western peace movement. It even seems that a certain kind of old-style Communist ideologist feels *more* secure when confronting his old-style mirror-opposite—some Western warrior embattled like the heroic Mr Heseltine across the Berlin Wall. All that has the comfort of the familiar: the script is known by rote. But the Western peace movement proposes unknown and sensitive problems and is received with a deep sense of threat.

I said a few pages back that pro-Soviet apologists might have a strong case, but one which may only be expressed *sotto voce*, if at all. The situation on the other side has become so screwed up, and in several different ways, that the infection of peace, in certain circumstances, actually could be de-stabilising. And, in the present posture of NATO, any 'de-stabilisation' to the East would be seized upon as a sign of Communist 'weakness', and would be exploited to NATO's advantage. This would probably induce the hardest-line reactions from the insecure Communist apparatus, and could lead on to enhanced bloc confrontation and enhanced internal repression. In short, any meddlesome attempts by Western peace movements to export the 'third way' to the East could blow up in their own faces; they could set in motion a chain of events which led to the opposite outcome.

This is not a stupid argument. In the politics of peace it is the most sensitive place of all, and in the coming years the most critical problems of both strategy and theory will lie in this area. No-one can foresee how things will work out, no-one has the expertise to foretell internal developments. But certain general observations may be offered.

First, some caution should be exercised before we accept this threatening term, 'de-stabilisation'. For the reigning incumbents of power any challenge to their authority will be perceived as 'de-stabilising'. Mrs Thatcher might find her authority 'de-stabilised' by a Freedom of Information Act or by a reproof from her bishops. Some experts on Soviet affairs (including Soviet citizens) advise that no extensive reforms are likely unless they are initiated from within the Party and from above. Even so, the mechanisms of reform are obscure, and will involve intense faction-fighting between interest-groups. And if reforms promise to be extensive as, for example, in the first years of Khrushchev, a great many powerful and comfortable people might find their positions to be threatened: not only hawks in the Politbureau and officials of the KGB, but also their deferential subordinates such as the learned Thebans of the State University of Tyumen. All these people will set up a great squawking that not only their jobs and patronage but also the Soviet state itself is being 'de-stabilised', and laid open to the aggressive designs of Western imperialism. What this emphasises is that the clipping of the wings of power is a necessary and normal objective of the peace movement, in the East as in the West, and that an outcry about 'de-stabilisation' could be the last refuge of the cold war scoundrels on both sides.

There could be, in the Soviet Union, a very much more untidy political scenario. This is a society which is, by any reckoning, long overdue for rationalisation and reform and most of the Soviet public knows it. Soviet life is tied up into dozens of knots, in part (but only in part) because of the protraction through decades of the cold war. The incumbent Soviet rulers need the cold war, and the siege mentality that goes with it, to hold their own ramshackle rule together. But in Russian history—way back into time, and before the Soviet Union was invented—'Westernising' influences have often been a precipitant of change. It is not impossible that the influence of the Western peace movement (which cannot plausibly be seen as the threatening Other) could precipitate an extensive thaw in culture and ideology, especially among the younger generation.

I will not attempt to foretell what contradictory ideological and political events might follow. But one thing is very clear. This will not be the moment for President Reagan (or his successor) to hurry forward new instalments of weaponry, nor for Western warriors to seek to take advantage of Soviet confusion by poking around in Soviet affairs and by beaming advice on Radio Liberty. They will of course attempt to meddle, and that is why it will be the first duty of the Western peace movement—not to meddle on its own accord—but to exert all its influence upon Western governments to meet a Soviet thaw with concession, reconciliation and measures of disarmament. If that could be done, then what might be 'de-stabilised' would be the cold war itself.

There is, secondly, a more serious possibility of 'de-stabilisation'. While this is improbable in the Soviet Union, successive episodes of 'instability' and 'normalisation' appear to be the norm in Eastern and Central Europe. And however clearly we may set out, as a theoretical proposition, the 'third way' of peace, in the real political world all social and intellectual forces are subject to the gravitational pull of the 'two sides'. As soon as any element detaches itself from one pole, it senses the tug of the other. The cold war, like a patrolling involuntary moon, pulls the tides of politics now to the West, now to the East.

All this was clear in the case of Poland. If the strategy of dialogue and of 'recognition' between the Western peace movement and autonomous social movements in the East was to be tested, surely the huge spaces forced open by Solidarity afforded abundant opportunity? Yet Poland has seemed to be, in the matter of peace, the lemon in the basket of oranges. It is not even true that the strategy was attempted and failed. It was never put to serious trial.

One comment on this record will be found in my exchange with Timothy Garton Ash in 1982 in the *Spectator*. Mr Ash has now returned to his criticisms in the final chapter of his study, *The Polish Revolution* (1983), which is a serious essay in political analysis. His challenge to the peace movement, and more especially to END and to myself, is not unfair. Yet it involves misunderstandings and misrecognitions which must take us into parish-pump matters.

Ash notes the remarkable simultaneity of the emergence of Solidarity and of peace movements in 1980–1. Yet 'these two apparently parallel movements showed remarkably *little* interest in each other. Most western peace campaigners did not see their struggle against cruise and Pershing II missiles as being linked to, let alone conditional upon, Solidarity's struggle'. A 'rare exception' was British END. Yet he implies that END's interest was largely rhetorical and for the record. A 'leading member of the international relations department attached to the National Commission of Solidarnosc in Gdansk' has informed him that END never formally approached Solidarity's leadership, and 'there had been almost no approaches from any of the western peace movements'. And she added: 'I think they were afraid of what they might find.'

But Mr Ash is trying to have his argument both ways. On the one hand, he explains (correctly) that Solidarity 'deliberately kept the whole area of defence and foreign policy off the agenda' because any intervention into such sensitive issues would have damaged the possibilities of a 'peaceful compromise' with the Polish regime. Solidarity was not a peace movement and it did not (until its final Congress) express any views on armaments. On the other hand, western peace movements are chided for not entering into some kind of formal diplomatic relations with the Hotel Morski in Gdansk—relations which, as we knew very well both from Solidarity's public positions and our own private enquiries, had not been invited and might be unwelcome.

The formality of Ash's language disguises the incoherence of organisations and the pace of events. For most of the time the 'international relations department attached to the National Commission' at Gdansk was a small group of translators working amidst hubbub and with little experience of the West; when a letter arrived belatedly, in a pile of post, from Len Murray, the General Secretary of the British TUC, 'the first reaction was: "Who's he? What's that?" ' (John Taylor, *Five Months with Solidarity*, p. 6). And of course: how could it have been otherwise? And, on the other side, 'western peace movements', which could bring out 'millions' onto the streets, sound like very heavy pieces of furniture, whereas they were movements made up of five parts of mood and of consciousness and one part of organisation. None of them had the resources to send formal delegations on speculative visits, nor to send ambassadors to present their credentials at Solidarity's Court of St. James. In Britain, CND, which is certainly open to criticism for insularity, did not appoint an international worker until the end of 1984; and END, in 1981, had 1½ full-time workers, deluged with work, and the most slender resources for travel. Moreover—and this is of general importance—END, as a point of principle, does not offer to intervene or to 'organise' on the other side. Dialogue, yes; interference, no.

In the early days of Solidarity the Institute for Workers Control (which is closely associated with the Russell Peace Foundation) attempted to send a formal delegation which would have included members of END Committee. The attempt was perhaps too high-profile, and visas were refused. In the next year several distinct attempts were made to interest pro-Solidarnosc weeklies or presses in publishing the END Appeal. The suggestions were always turned down. The message that came back to us, loud and clear, was that Solidarity did not wish to enter into relations with peace movements and might indeed find these compromising. In these circumstances British and other western peace activists visited Poland low-profile and on their own free enterprise—not as ambassadors to the Hotel Morski but simply as supporters of peace, trade unionism and civil rights. They always met with a ready welcome; but they also discovered, to their dismay, that—in Mr Ash's words—'a great many Solidarity supporters privately thought the western peace movement was a bad thing, because it tended to weaken the West's resistance to Soviet imperialism'.

It is a record of non-communication and misrecognition. In our view, Solidarity had proclaimed that it was a trade-union movement *only*, and therefore it was the first responsibility of Western trades-union and Labour movements to make a response. Some of us did our best to press forward this mutual recognition, but the British response was sluggish and inadequate and (but this is another story) the advisors of Solidarity and KOR in exile did not always appear to wish that this recognition should take place. Meanwhile it became daily more clear that the Polish renewal *was* a peace question. On the one hand, it signalled an opening towards the East and a crumblihg of the blocs, and Solidarnosc badges multiplied at western peace demonstrations. On the other hand, the ominous preparations for Soviet or Warsaw Pact intervention threatened the entire peace project. It was emphatically a time when Solidarity (and KOR) and the peace movements should have found time for dialogue with each other.

I am certainly willing to accept that the Western peace movement merits some of Solidarity's and Mr Ash's criticisms. But I cannot accept that misrecognitions were only on the western side, nor can I accept the argument as presented in Ash's terms. For he writes (of Solidarity's leadership):

> At first, they recognised as western 'allies' almost anyone who declared themselves as 'allies'. Later, they became more discriminating about their western supporters. They did not particularly recognise the western peace movement as an ally because the western peace movement did not particularly distinguish itself as an ally, by vocal or practical support where it mattered. They were

> more inclined to recognise in the initials NATO an ally, because the voice of NATO was actually heard loud and clear, for example in December 1980, warning the Soviet Union against armed intervention. If 300,000 people had marched through the streets of Bonn to warn the Soviets against intervention, as they did in October 1981 to protest against NATO's new Pershing II and cruise missiles, then Solidarity members might have begun to think seriously about their nearest western counterparts.

There is something right in this passage and there is something wrong. If I attend to what is wrong, it is because this illustrates how misrecognitions arise (which still continue and will recur). I take it that Mr Ash is saying that 'at first' (1980?) Solidarity was open to any kind of alliances with the West, but that 'later' (by 1981?) the leadership was tipping in its interests towards NATO. He does not explain what 'practical support' Solidarity hoped to obtain from peace movements whose approaches it did not wish to receive. So far as 'vocal support', Solidarity was very probably not in any position to know what support it had. The West German peace movement could not have mounted 300,000 people in the streets of Bonn in December 1980, because, as we have seen (p. 13), as a mass movement it did not arrive on the scene until October 1981. At that great Bonn demonstration, the question of peace and Poland very certainly found vocal expression. I was present at that huge meeting, and perhaps no speaker met with a warmer reception than Erhard Eppler, who declared, to immense applause, 'Any Soviet intervention in Poland affects us all.'*

Two weeks later I was a speaker at CND's rally of some quarter-of-a-million in Hyde Park, and declared: 'We must demand upon both NATO and the Warsaw powers—no intervention in either Greece or Poland. Let Poland be Polish and let Greece be Greek!' Once again the huge crowd responded with applause. Similar messages went out from the great

* 'Wir feiern hierzulande den Mut der Polen, die sich nicht mehr vorschreiben lassen wollen, wie sie zu leben haben. Ist es so schlimm, wenn wir uns nicht vorschreiben lassen wollen, wie wir zu sterben haben? Die Europäiserung Europas findet nicht nur an der Weichsel statt, sondern auch am Rhein. Das bedeutet auch: Eine sowjetische Intervention in Polen träfe uns alle.' (*Bonn 10.10.81*, p. 114.)

Amsterdam demonstration a week later, and no doubt from other capitals, and it is difficult to know how we could have been more 'vocal' than that.

This was very late in the day. The Kremlin may not have been impressed by these vocal offerings, nor by the many that had preceded them. But the *Daily Telegraph* was, and it editorialised (October 26, 1981): 'Mr Brezhnev would long since have sent in the Red Army to crush Solidarity had he not feared that the gruesome spectacle would stop the now, for him, almost unbelievably promising European "Peace" movement in its tracks.' It is conceivable that Western peace voices were among the field of political forces which enforced a 'Polish' solution instead of a far more terrible re-enactment of Hungarian and Czechoslovak experience. But, if so, how was Solidarity to know that our voices were raised? Do they know now? The official Communist media in Poland will certainly have suppressed this part of our message (while enlarging all parts critical of NATO). And neither Radio Free Europe nor the Voice of America will have gone out of their way to correct them.

By October 1981 the movements may have been within reach of mutual recognition. But it was already too late. Influential hands had been extended from the West to Solidarity, but (in my own experience) we never received any firm hand-clasp in return. This was not only because Solidarity wished to keep its hands out of sensitive areas. It was also because Solidarity, in its foreign relations, had become sucked within the tidal tug of that patrolling moon, the cold war, and had come, as Ash says, to 'recognise in the initials NATO an ally'. Moreover, all the resources for ready communication lay on that side. The 'voice of NATO' could be heard 'loud and clear', even through the Polish static, because it could be projected by multiple loud-hailers. The peace movement had no 'Radio Peace', few foreign correspondents or expense-account emissaries who could flit to and fro. And in many Western nations the role of spokespersons and prime defenders of Solidarity had been taken over by first and second generation emigré Poles, deeply embittered by prior experiences of betrayal, fiercely hostile to 'the Left', and in some cases actual advocates of the 'roll back' of 'Yalta', by military force. The substantial Solidarity headquarters in the expensive heart of Washington proclaims not only the loyalty of the vast American–Polish community, but also the assimilation of this loyalty to a Reaganish view of the world.

A few days after the proclamation of martial law I attended the most mournful political event of my life: a demonstration of protest called in Hyde Park. It was a day as bitter and cold as were our hearts. I felt shame at the small numbers—a few thousand only—picking their way through the ice and turning up their collars against the wind. The scene seemed to symbolise the return of the cold war, just as the scene of CND's great demonstration in the same place only eight weeks before had symbolised the promise of thaw. There was a good scattering of CND badges: not nearly enough, but at least the peace activists turned out better than the multitude of our critics, who in the warmth of their homes had become Solidarity supporters overnight and were laughing at us through their lace curtains.

I think that the meeting had been set up in the wrong way, although the organisers were doing their best. Surely, on the declaration of martial law against Solidarnosc, the immediate mass protest should have been called by the British trade unions, with political parties and the peace movement giving support? I do not know what mixture of lethargy or factionalism, insularity or timidity, had deprived Solidarity of its obvious partner's support. But it was one more sign that the tide, both within Poland and without, was swinging to the West. The meeting had a cross-party platform, and one or two speakers made scarcely-veiled incitements to war against the Soviet Union. I spoke (as requested) on the peace movement's behalf, and at the first mention of 'peace' incurred the barracking and abuse of the ethnic Poles who pressed around the platform. We then formed ourselves into a melancholy crocodile, with the Poles singing again and again and again, as if it were a lament over the dead, Żeby Polska, and we trooped off to the Polish Embassy. It had become a Polish, and not a British, protest.

It was now the turn of President Reagan to say, 'Let Poland be Poland', not at Hyde Park, but on prime-time TV. Solidarity's pinioned body was laved by Western rhetorical tides. No doubt some of Solidarity's supporters accepted the NATO basket of bluster, bluff and boycott in the instrumental spirit in which it was intended. It was not for their own but for Russian consumption. (As British officers used to say in World War II, in the privacy of the officers' mess, of the alliance with the Soviet Union against Hitler: 'Any stick will do to beat a dirty dog.') But, as Mr Ash himself has testified, Mr Reagan became popular with many in Warsaw and remains so to this day. This is more than a matter of misrecognition, and it is absurd to suppose that it does not present difficulties to the Western peace movement. The difficulties have extended into the domestic political life of some nations, where support for Solidarity has become a football kicked between small leftist sects and the conservative Right. In the extensive opinion in the middle (which includes much of the Labour, trade union and peace movements, and especially the young) a deep respect for Solidarity is nourished which has never found effective expression; people feel that the radical young Solidarity activists 'blew it' in the final months (but they were driven into a corner), that they never responded to the voices of the peace movement (but they may never have heard these), but that it is a movement of hope and honour which must arise again.

I spoke again, on the peace movement's behalf, at another demonstration in Hyde Park in August 1982. The attendance was even smaller, with no winter weather as excuse. There were few CND flashes to be seen. This time the hostility of those around the platform stood up against me like a wall. For some, the mere mention of 'peace' was an obscenity. I learned that the very invitation of a speaker from the peace movement onto the platform almost provoked a split in the organising committee. But, as a gentle sign that some communication was still possible, one elderly Pole separated himself from his fellows and came to shake my hand: 'I do not agree with what you are saying, but I thank you for coming.'

I remember this because it has not been often in the past few years that a Pole has shaken my hand. The personal experiences which I have sketched are perhaps not unrepresentative. In the past three years (1982–4) a little dialogue has developed; offices of Solidarnosc in exile have signed common statements with sections of the peace movement; their representatives have spoken at END Conventions; individual Solidarity exiles have found (perhaps to their surprise) that they have met with a warm welcome as speakers with the Greens, the Italian Communists, at CND branches, at CND's annual Glastonbury Festival. In Poland itself we have passed through a most melancholy period of failed communication. The majority of Poles who, for deep historical reasons, love the Russians rather less than the Irish love the British, retired within the stockade of their national and Catholic culture: any enemy of the Russians was a friend of theirs. Since the peace movement was presented to them by their media as pro-Soviet—or at least 'soft' on the Soviets—then it must be their enemy.

As a criticism of a lopsidedness in some parts of the Western movements this had some validity—most notably in regard to the silence of some West Germans. But it was not a criticism which took rational or constructive forms. I have learned from published and from private accounts that in the aftermath of martial law extraordinary fantasies of war or 'liberation' disturbed the public mind. Lawrence Weschler reports (of the last months of 1981),

> The scenario I was frequently offered conjured up a Russian army bogged down in Poland for months, maybe years, of bloody guerrilla fighting, while one by one the other Warsaw Pact countries—whose armies, incidentally, would likewise be detailed on Polish soil—would become engulfed in working class rebellions of their own, rebellions that would eventually spread into the Soviet Union itself, leading to the collapse of the Kremlin regime.
>
> (*Solidarity*, 1982, p. 220.)

Mr Ash also acknowledges the spread of messianic visions, as in the aftermath of other thwarted revolutionary impulses:

the chiliasm of despair. Returning to Poland in late 1982, Weschler found such fantasies endemic. Talking with a village priest and longtime 'activist', he asked:

> 'So what do you think is going to happen?' He leaned forward and quietly said, 'A miracle,' rolling his eyes toward Heaven and smiling. I . . . leaned forward and asked, 'Like what?' He leaned even closer, his face now a mixture of anticipation and serenity, and whispered, confidentially, 'The Third World War'.
>
> (*The Passion of Poland*, Pantheon, 1984, p. 170.)

With extraordinary and self-disciplined non-violence the masses who were Solidarnosc had attempted a Polish renewal until they confronted the limits of the possible. The response had been martial law. In their bitterness many turned not against the immediate agents of their repression—the army and the Party's *nomenklatura*—but against the forces which imposed those limits: the Russians, the historic enemy. And who could aid them against the Russians? Only the United States, the 'West'. Passion projected absurd irrationalities. In a Third World War somehow 'the missiles will sail over us in both directions, but we will be left unscathed' (Weschler, *op. cit.*, p. 171).* In more rational-seeming terms many Poles accepted the symbolism of NATO weapons as their own 'defence'; in some never-explained way, cruise and Pershing

---

* Among such notions still canvassed in Poland is that of a writer ('We Must Build an Ark before the Flood') in the *Biuletyn Dolnoslaski* (Lower Silesian Bulletin), March 1984. This offers the following scenario for a war between NATO and the Warsaw Pact: day two to four, a front is established near the Elbe, where Soviet and GDR armies engage with NATO: day four, Polish regular forces strike the Soviet army in its rear (Soviet army disintegrates). Meanwhile Polish reservists and irregulars attack Soviet reinforcements moving through Poland to front, and (with the aid of the Polish regulars returning victorious from the front) 'hold back the Soviet drive. . . until the NATO forces arrive.' As for nukes, NATO plans 'envisage a particularly heavy bombardment of Poland. . . aimed at checking the armed Soviet millions proceeding towards the Elbe. . . However, maybe NATO's plans would change if it were known that an uprising would erupt in Poland'. It seems that some Poles will still entertain any crack-brained fantasy, no matter how bloodthirsty and self-centred, rather than pursue the same objectives (greater Polish autonomy and democracy) in alliance with Western peace forces.

missiles (some of which will be targeted on Poland) were visualised as a protective net extending to Poland's eastern borders and keeping the Russians out.

This was scarcely fertile ground for dialogue with peace movements. And some of the intellectual communicators, the internationally-minded circles of KOR (and then of KOS), were throughout 1982 and 1983 in prison where no communication was possible. Moreover, there may have been theoretical reasons why KOR/KOS had not been disposed to enter dialogue. A founding document of what was to become KOR's position was Jacek Kuron and Karel Modzelewski's *An Open Letter to the Party* of 1965.* Although many of their views had been modified by 1980, perhaps this response to nuclear weapons remained unrevised? Nuclear weapons (they then said) were 'a modern addition to the traditional arsenal of anti-revolutionary arguments'.

> Today, when the stocks of nuclear weapons are more than enough to destroy the world, the governing elites of the two great blocs which share power in the world decry revolution as a crime against internal peace and humanity. Those who possess the arsenals filled with the means of nuclear annihilation. . . demand obedience from the masses in the name of avoiding a world-wide nuclear war.

But (Kuron and Modzelewski then went on):

> A world nuclear conflict would be absurd from the point of view of the goals of both great blocs; it would lead to the destruction, if not of the whole of mankind, at least of the major powers. . . It would be suicide. The two great blocs do not want mutual destruction in any case, but are engaged in an economic, political and diplomatic competition based upon a division into spheres of influence. In their struggle against revolutionary movements, atomic weapons are a means of blackmail.

And a reference to the views of the 'Chinese bureaucracy' suggested that they shared Mao's view that nuclear weapons

* First published in English in the American *New Politics*, Vol. 5, nos. 2 & 3. Reproduced in part (without explanation of origin) in Tariq Ali (ed.), *New Revolutionaries* (1969).

were a 'paper tiger'.

The view that nuclear weapons are an instrument of blackmail and of internal discipline, but could never be used since their use would be plainly irrational and against the interests of any ruling elite is, of course, widely held also in the West. It shores up some theories of 'deterrence'. I do not credit it because I do not consider that history has ever been cut out of that kind of rational, self-interested cloth. But the evidence as to an irrational acceleration in the arms race may have been slow to get through to Poland, where, in any case, the active circle of KOR was submerged in other preoccupations. It seems to me possible that this old scepticism as to the threat of nuclear war—and suspicion of it as a form of Soviet-sponsored blackmail against any popular movements designated as 'destabilising'—may have underscored KOR's suspicion of the Western peace movement.

A dialogue of a kind is now starting. Poles are not always easy to understand. Absolutists in argument, in political practice they arrive at ambiguous compromises. Violent in mutual recriminations, they respond to real domestic violence with abhorrence. Even in the worst post-war purges, the Polish Stalinists did not often shoot their victims. The murder of Father Jerzy Popieluszko caused a national trauma, whereas the murder of Pio la Torre was for some North Italians (but not for Sicilians) just one more example of Mafia norms.* In no other Communist country whatsoever could Lech Walesa still be half-free and taking his lunch to work. For this reason one must learn to endure with good-humour the furious Polish-centric arguments of the past two or three years, in which the problems of Europe and the

* Pio la Torre, leader of the Sicilian region of the Italian Communist Party, was murdered by the Mafia in Palermo on April 30th, 1982, after he had taken a leading part in the campaign against the cruise missile base at Comiso: see Ben Thompson, *Comiso* (END Special Report), pp. 12-13. In England more recently there have been suggestions that an elderly woman in Shropshire, Miss Hilda Murrell, an active anti-nuclear campaigner, may have been murdered 'accidentally' by intelligence snoopers. All that we can be certain of, in this democratic country, is that, whatever the truth is, it will remain an 'official secret'.

world must always be measured against the Polish imperative. It is usual for such arguments to by-pass the stage of attempted reason and to move directly into savage and contemptuous sarcasm or into a polemical lunge at the throat.

There is also a moral stridency to be expected from men and women who walk always within the shadow of prison. This gives them a licence to abuse, in the knowledge that in our safety we will suffer abuse in silence. We are informed that the overriding threat comes from Soviet totalitarianism, and that the Soviet Union menaces West Europe with military blackmail, and that they *know* that this is true since, unlike us, they have suffered this truth in their own persons. We are accused of nourishing 'the spirit of Munich'. (Such accusations, like similar charges of 'appeasement' in a letter to me from the pseudonymous Czech, Václav Racek, are industriously extracted in Conservative Party HQ and sent out with their speaker's notes.) There is even, on occasion, a hint of moral blackmail. They are risking themselves every day (as they are): why will the Western peace movement, in its comfortable freedom, not 'risk' itself in their support? The first common task is to stop the 'expansion of tyranny from the East into the West'—

> And this means paying a certain price. We are fully willing to pay our part of that price and it is a sad fact that, apparently, the free people are not.
>
> ('Letter from KOS', *END Journal*, 11, August-September 1984.)

Dear friends in Solidarity or KOS, if any of you should read these pages! We submit. We do not enter any moral contest. We honour your commitment, and we would not dream of weighing our own in the same scales of 'risk'. It is true that many in the Western peace movements have, as a result of non-violent actions, briefly visited prisons; and for many women these visits are repeating and becoming longer. But for many of us our commitment involves us in few risks, save those of ridicule and of the expense of spirit and life. So let us take your moral case as won.

Yet what 'price' are we failing to pay? What 'risk' would

we take if we endorsed, without examination, every one of your assertions? Can you really suppose that we are nervous of incurring the displeasure of Mr Zhukov and the Soviet authorities? We have incurred this already. Do you suppose that those who publish, in the pages of *Commentary* or *Encounter*, declamations against the overriding threat of Soviet totalitarianism incur (if they live in the West) any risk whatsoever? On the contrary, if we were to subscribe our own names to these declamations we would be rewarded with the applause of the Western establishment. What we would place at risk would be rationality, for the sake of placing our impeccable moral credentials upon exhibition.

Yes, we live in the 'free world', although the air of freedom becomes more rarified year by year. The flow of information available to us is greater than can be found in Warsaw. We have sought—as you would do if you were here—to put our freedoms to use. It is our measured view that the cold war cannot be blamed upon one side only, but is a reciprocal, mutually-reinforcing process. We do not share your view that Soviet military power is a present menace to the West; on the contrary, recent experience, not least in Poland, suggests increasing weakness on the Soviet side. We regard all measures of militarisation as enhancing our common dangers, blocking the escape-routes to the future, and that their 'price' will beggar imagination. We consider that, together, we should be defining the positions of a third way, detached from the tug of the cold war's tides.

In this we may be wrong. But we must address the matter not in hectoring moralisms but in rational terms. Solidarity encountered, at the end of 1981, the limits of the Communist and cold war 'possible'. It also encountered the limits of an argument which has recently been presented by Mihailo Markovič, the independent Yugoslav Marxist philosopher:

> The liberation of Eastern Europe can only be the work of Eastern Europeans—to be sure with the support of all those who resist every kind of oppression. This liberation will take a lot of time, it will require enormous moral strength, risk and sacrifice.
>
> (*END Journal*, 12, October-November 1984.)

This argument has my profound assent: not only can liberation not be brought from without, but the attempt to do so will enforce repression. Yet how can we offer this argument to a Pole? For the majority of the nation, in most disciplined and non-provocative ways, attempted non-violent self-liberation, with a display of 'enormous moral strength, risk and sacrifice'. And the answer was *nyet*. With their heads smashed against these stony limits, is it not inevitable that some Poles should search for dramatic alternatives: perhaps 'a miracle'?

Solidarity's Western admirers have searched in the same way. Timothy Garton Ash has candidly argued that 'I believe the United States would be morally justified in using force to help the Poles defeat General Jaruzelski—if that were possible without risking a war in Europe and a nuclear holocaust, which of course it is not.' (*N Y Review of Books*, November 22, 1984). No doubt many Poles think the same. Many Westerners might feel such a cause to be morally just (as they did fifty years ago in Spain), but I have already expressed my nausea at the assumption by the United States of such an imperial 'moral mission'. If President Reagan wishes to be cast as Lord Byron at Missolonghi, then I hope that he will go back to Hollywood and play the part on a silent movie. And, as Ash agrees, this option has been closed by the realities of modern war. What other options do he and his friends, offer?

Mr Ash, in a tentative counterfactual essay in 'missed opportunity' (*The Polish Revolution*, pp. 324–330), suggests that Solidarity's positions might have been held open if 'the West' (that is, certain Western governments and banks) had promoted early in 1981 an imaginative 'Marshall Plan' of some 20 billion dollars, tied to a series of hidden and not-so-hidden conditions. In return for these credits, 'the West' would have demanded guarantees of Solidarity's independent status, would have demanded the full disclosure of information on the Polish economy to 'the West', would have dictated extensive reorganisation of Polish industry, and would have explored the possibility of channelling aid in preference to private agriculture and (if direct aid) through the Church. In short, 'the West' (or certain Western governments and banks) would have used this 'Marshall Plan' as a gentle instrument of weakening the Polish authorities and privatising sectors of the economy.

It is not difficult to see that Mr Ash, bumping his head against the same limits of the possible, has come up with a fantasy of his own. There might be circumstances in which a Polish government would buy its way out of crisis with Western credits even upon unfavourable conditions. But these circumstances certainly did not exist in 1981–3, when the blocs were entering a major contest of 'face' about intermediate nuclear weapons, and when Pershing IIs were rising on the West German horizon. Neither Mr Ash nor his Polish friends can rationally suppose that, in the prevailing terms of East–West confrontation, the Communist authorities (or 'the Russians') would have tolerated a Western essay in graduated destabilisation and privatisation.

What might, conceivably, have been tolerated would have been Solidarity's survival in return for a package of aid accompanied by some major Western concession. And that concession could have come only in the most sensitive area of all: the nuclear and ideological confrontation. 'The West' might have bought the continued existence of above-ground Solidarity for the cancellation of Pershing II missiles. And, then, not only would Poland have been freer but both Poland and West Germany would have been more secure. The only rational options open, within the domain of possibility, lay in some bargain which traded some real measure of Western disarmament in return for the consolidation of Polish freedoms. Polish self-liberation is only possible within the larger politics of peace.

Some of us in the peace movement have said this insistently, before martial law and since. The best place for Western concession (we have argued) would be in reductions of the militarisation of West Germany. This leads on to a reconsideration of Rapacki-type solutions, linking West Germany with the GDR, Poland and Czechoslovakia, leading on from a nuclear-free zone to mutual reductions in conventional arms, and the increasing opening of frontiers to the flow of persons and ideas. Everything has been going in the opposite direction, and, in consequence, the Polish situation is getting worse.

A serious dialogue on such a common strategy has scarcely yet been opened with our Polish friends.* It has been refused, on occasion, for trivial reasons. Because, some twenty-five years ago, Rapacki-type solutions were, in very different circumstances, favoured by Communist governments, they must for that reason be a Communist trick which cannot be enlarged into a third way of peace. Or it has been refused, in terms of an emotional utopian absolutism. Poland must either be 'free'—to the point that Poland may opt, if it wishes, to join NATO—or any intermediate station is an insult to the Polish nation.

Mr Lawrence Weschler has perhaps conveyed to some Polish friends that I have been offering this kind of insult. For he quotes 'a well-known British peace activist and historian' (guess who?) as 'commenting' on the 'unbridled nationalism of the Poles' and as warning the citizens of East European nations that 'even following extensive loosening of their internal totalitarian political systems, their countries must still remain within the Soviet sphere of influence—somewhat like Finland'.

I gather that my supposed views (as presented by Weschler) may have got back to some persons in KOS, who have taken the greatest offence. So E.P. Thompson—or 'the Western peace movement'—wish to turn Poland into another Finland!!! Let me rehearse my published views once more. I have argued for the perspective of an 'Austrian solution' for Europe, with the mutually agreed withdrawal of Soviet and American forces from Europe, East and West. I have argued also that, in the shorter run, the 'Finlandisation' of Western Europe is less likely than the 'Finlandisation' of some nations in Eastern Europe: that is, the Soviet presence

* There is a suggestion that such a dialogue may now be beginning: notably, in Jacek Kuron's *Open Letter to All People in the World who care about Peace* (June, 1984). But Kuron wishes to enlist the peace movement in support of his Polish strategies: he does not yet see it as an equal partner, working towards common strategies.

and hegemony might be loosened, and greater autonomy be gained, in response to Western concessions. I have argued that we will not get out of the cold war confrontation in one sudden flip-over but down a gradient; and that, as intermediate way-stations, the increasing 'Finlandisation' of the East and 'Swedenisation' of West Europe, is to be both worked for and welcomed.

It would be nice if Poland were to be 'free' tomorrow, although it would be less nice if Poles were to take their place in NATO's councils. But neither is going to happen, this side of a 'miracle'. Meanwhile, Finland is not a terrible place, nor as trussed-up and terrified as *Encounter* polemicists pretend; and if I suggest that the route to Polish freedom might be through the Finland station, this ought not to occasion a lunge at my throat. The mistake is to suppose that if a nation escapes from one sphere of influence it must at once join the other: only-two-sides. But the third way of peace must be working—and working together, East and West—for the withering away of *both* spheres of influence and an enlarging space of autonomy in-between. It may be that Adam Michnik of KOS has glimpsed this possibility when he writes that it is 'not unthinkable that a spectacular peaceful solution in Poland will become the starting point for the resolution of international tensions' (Weschler, *op. cit.*, p. 248). But to achieve this peaceful solution will require the common efforts of Solidarity and of the Western peace movement, with all their associated political forces and cultural resources. It will not be brought by NATO bluster nor bought by Western banks. For what some risk-taking friends in Poland *still* will not understand is that 'the West' (in this form) is concerned not in the least with the advantage of the Polish people. It is concerned with exploiting perceived 'weaknesses' (for the Polish renewal appeared only in its aspect as Communist 'weakness' to them) and in furthering NATO's advantage against the Warsaw bloc.

I commenced this digression on the matter of Poland from a consideration of the question of 'destabilisation'. I have agreed that there were misrecognitions between the peace movement and Solidarity, and that an opportunity was lost. But nothing in this argument lends any support to the view that the strategy of the peace movement is an agent of destabilisation. On the contrary, Polish repression and the consequent and continuing risks of real (and bloody) destabilisation arise precisely because the strategy of the peace movement has *not* been taken. The third way of peace is not just one desirable option. It is the only way out.

There are still those in the Western peace movement who advise keeping all these considerations (which they describe as 'human rights') in a 'pending' file. Yes, they would like to see all these 'human rights'. But realism dictates a two-stage programme, like the lift-off of a space rocket. First must come disarmament (where the onus lies with the West). Second, there will follow, as light follows day, a period of detente, in which ideological hostilities will soften and some democratisation will ensue on the other side.

These arguments are well-intended but they lack the realism to which they aspire. Detente, in the early seventies, did not favour democratisation: least of all in the USSR and Czechoslovakia. And those dreadful people, Soviet citizens or Czechs or Poles, who are suffering their own domestic abuses, will make their own decisions and move in their own ways. They will not wait about compliantly until such moment as a Western committee (perhaps meeting in Boston or in the Friends Meeting House on Euston Road) looks at its watch, and signals to them that the second stage of democratic lift-off may now, with due sobriety, begin.

Those dreadful people will act impulsively and untidily and without consultation, and make trouble for us. But they will not only make trouble. They will see openings towards peace which we, with our western perceptions, can never see. They will contribute new themes to our understanding, as 'dialogue' and 'trust' have done. They will greatly enrich the theoretical content of the 'third way', and stand the theory on two legs instead of one. This now is going forward, in Moscow, in Budapest, and in the circles of Charter 77 in Prague. The most perspicacious essay on the perspective of 'a democratic peace' has come, not from a Western pen, but from a Czech: Dr Jaroslav Šabata in *Voices from Prague*.

The most eloquent plea for the peaceful Europeanisation of Europe has come from a Hungarian: György Konrád in *Antipolitics.*

The two-stage lift-off theory will not work in that form. It is wrong to say that 'human rights' must be a precondition of disarmament: that way we will get neither. It is wrong to say that 'human rights' will be the consequence of disarmament: our friends on the other side have not given us power-of-attorney to make that decision. Both must take place together, as part of one single process, the making of a democratic peace.

This is not to say that this little formula will disperse all complexities. If the forty-year-old ' nots of the cold war begin to be cut things will fall apart in unpredictable ways. There will be political lurches, in both West and East. Western nations may attempt their own social transitions, or may (Spain, Greece) decide to get out of NATO. In the East there may be new renewals and Springs. As a matter of course, the hard men of NATO and the Warsaw Pact will do all in their power to extract advantage for their own side. We have seen that Mr Zhukov is in the extraction business with the Western peace movement now. And it is clear that the opaque think-tanks of Washington are bubbling with powerful thoughts as to whether or how far independent peace initiatives in the East might be exploited to the advantage of Uncle Sam. A learned Theban, an analyst in the Policy bureau of the US Department of Defense—a man so close to the sweaty armpits of power that he must enter the caveat that 'the views expressed here do not necessarily reflect those of the US government'—has recently surveyed the 'Eastern European Doves' (Robert English in *Foreign Policy*, 56, Fall 1984):

> The United States should keep quiet and allow the East and West European peace movements to support each other as natural allies in their struggle against the military policies of both superpowers. For however unequal it seems and however threatening the West European peace movements appear to NATO, the greater threat is to the Soviets.

It is good to know that the United States will 'keep quiet' for a while, and permit us to do our own thing, although we should remember that there are other agencies, with sweatier armpits, which do not feel bound to follow official governmental briefs. (They are rather active in Nicaragua today.) But I think that the analysis of our learned Theban is wrong. What the growth of an independent peace movement over there will do is 'threaten', not the 'Soviets', but the whole rationale of the cold war. What it will strengthen, immeasurably, is the third way of peace.

Yet that cold involuntary moon will still patrol, tugging the tides of politics this way and that. As we watch new friends appear at our front we must still take care to watch our backs, where the true destabilisers of the Two Sides will seek to exploit to their own advantage the motions for peace in the Other.

In my view we should search together, not from some sudden cancellation of 'Yalta', but for a more gentle gradient in which disarmament and the opening of human communications go together. Western peace movements have no brief to interfere or to 'change the social system' in the East (as Mr Zhukov alleges). That is the business of the East's own citizens, if they so wish, just as political changes in the West are our own. But it is normal for us to welcome such advance, in any part of the world, of those rights of expression, access to information, and self-organisation without which the fluency of citizen communication is not possible.

I have written repeatedly about a 'healing-process' between the blocs. This cannot rest upon a neo-Leninist strategy in which 'vanguards' on both sides lock onto a common programme. While mutual solidarities inevitably will arise, our business should be not to draw this discourse into narrow channels but to throw it outwards to the widest public. Our discourse between the blocs, just as our discourse within our own nations, must be a plural discourse and a discourse of alliance. We must talk candidly with the officials, search out their doves, but break out of the captivity of conducted 'peace rituals and repressive hospitality.* We must talk candidly with the democratic opposition, not only about our agreements but about our disagreements. We should pursue the proposal of Charter 77, in its remarkable letter to the END Convention in Perugia (*END Journal*, 12 October-November 1984), of attempting round-table trialogues, in which officials, independents and Western movements meet together. And if the spaces for independent citizen initiatives in the East began to close in 1983–4, then in the immediate future we must press them open once again.

This is work, not only for those who wear badges and consider themselves to be activists for peace. It is work for all who wish to heal our human culture. It is work for orchestras, for scholars, for writers, for travellers, for young people and for their music. It is perhaps, most of all, work for the younger generations, on both sides, who do not bear the traumas of the past.

For some of us in the past five years it has seemed lonely work, which only a few scores or a few hundreds were doing. But the first openings in that 'iron curtain' have been made. We ask now for others to come and help us, not according to our directions, but finding their own openings in their own way. Fence-cutters of the world, unite!

If the work gathers way, the entire field-of-force of post-war international politics may be transformed. We may find that the dedicated operators of the cold war, despite their substantial resources, are fewer and less powerful than we supposed. But these are the true Iagos whom we may never forgive: those who seek to foul the springs of discourse: those who scurry from the West, in the masks of goodwill, to exposed persons in Prague or in Warsaw or in Moscow, conveying slander and seeking to twist dialogue to the tunes of NATO propaganda: those who, in the name of 'unity', seek to split the peace movement and turn a remnant to

* As any anthropologist can tell us, the host-guest relationship can be an unequal one of obligation and control. Communist states have developed the hosting of visiting delegations, with heavy constraints of protocol, to a fine art. The problem of transforming formal and invigilated exchanges into informal and open ones is now on our agenda.

Moscow's service. These operators endanger the future of the world far more than the hapless servitors of nuclear weapons, quietly yawning and rolling their joints, deep in the silos of Grand Forks, North Dakota or the Kola peninsula. It is not these bored young men but the ideologists with 'moral ends' who will send the missiles on their way.

Only one thing is certain: the world cannot go on as it is. We must make a new world, of new inter-nation and inter-bloc relations, or there will be no world at all. And I mean a new *world*, and not just a healed Europe. Today that cold patrolling moon is tugging the tides of cold war across the entire globe. It is the whole world which is threatened and which must be repaired, and the non-aligned peace movement must look for its allies everywhere.

This is not to say that the North–South contradiction, or the imperatives of the hungry half of the world, have displaced for us the political priority of healing the East/West confrontation. Indeed, a certain kind of flight into sentimental 'Third Worldism' could be an evasion of the responsibilities of the North. It is, precisely, the irrelevant aggressions of the East/West conflict which are now being exported wholesale to the South—quite literally exported in the atrocity of the arms trade, in the export of military infrastructures, in 'aid' given to juntas and debt-ridden tyrannies, in the contest for spheres of influence, and in the consequent screwing-up of political, economic and social life. Our duty to the South still demands that we heal the contradictions of the North. But the third way must become a global way.

I cannot find any sound reason for predicting the outcome. If I have a sense that the world may continue and may be renewed, I can support this by no more than the pricking in my thumbs. My sense, or 'suspicion', is shared by others, 'that the Iron Curtain is but a pile of decaying ideological rubbish, which has to be held upright by the extensive military hardware of the two blocs and by the mutual blackmail of the nuclear threat'. The words are those of Zdena Tomin (*New Statesman*, October 26, 1984), herself a former spokesperson of Charter 77 and now an involuntary exile in

Britain, whose resilience and wise advice has heartened us in our work of putting Europe back together.

I share her hope:

> That the human, social, historical, and in a true sense political, conditions for the crumble and fall of the Iron Curtain are here; that it is a workable dream.

V 'A SHIELD AGAINST CHAOS'

> Early in October, 1979, an 'expert' sort of young man came upon the BBC news, and informed us that we are to have 140 cruise missiles with nuclear warheads stationed on our soil. These are to be called Tomahawks, a reassuring cowboys-and-Indians sort of name. They are to be our 'contribution' to NATO. . .

I find this in an article which I wrote for *New Society* in December 1979. It comes with a sense of shock to realise that, for me and many others, the peace movement in its present form has now been in existence for five years.

An immense amount of life has been poured into that interval. What has that expense of spirit—those innumerable tramping feet, that milliard of public meetings and committees, that tonnage of correspondence and of publications, those frosty benders beneath the shadows of clattering helicopters—what has all this achieved?

If we ask this from the perspective of 'arms control', then the facile answer is 'nothing'. I said, at the CND demonstration in Hyde Park in October 1981: 'We have not yet stopped one missile in its tracks.' And we still have not yet stopped one.

In West Europe we were given a four year time-table to stop cruise and Pershing. The task became obsessional: it polarised the political life of nations, in which the peace movement contested, upon unequal terms, with the resources of established power. And we failed.

In the wake of that failure, the sharks' fins of the successor systems now cleave the waters. In Britain we have not stopped Trident nor the Tornado. America's sea and air-launched cruise missiles are entering deployment, and little pirate armadas (such as the *Iowa* task-force) are being prepared to support the rapid deployment forces. The MX is a-building. The Mediterranean (Sicily, Sardinia, Pantellaria) is being militarised. In the East the GDR and Czechoslovakia have been drawn into the nuclear-basing club, while Soviet cruise missiles are in advanced testing. The Atlantic and Pacific oceans are busy with the sharks' fins of both sides. Japan is under United States' pressure to rebuild its military forces. 'Conventional' armaments are being hyped up in Europe, not as an alternative but as an addition to nukes. And President Reagan's eyes are now set on the stars. . .

It would be easy to conclude that the rival military establishments will go ahead with their procurements despite whatever we can do, and that 'arms control' will only be a code-word for measures to control public opinion: that is, for controlling us. At the best, the peace movement has only forced the armourers to modify their rhetoric. We hear little these days about 'warning shots' or 'limited' nuclear war.

Yet if we ask the same question in political terms, then we get different answers. It is not true, even in immediate political terms, that the record of the past five years is one of unrelieved defeat. In the major heartlands of the Cold War, at the cost of the fierce polarisation of political life, the armourers have triumphed. This was signalled by the return to power in 1983 of Chancellor Kohl and of Mrs Thatcher; by the disciplinary controls imposed on the Warsaw bloc (notably the repression of Solidarnosc); and by the fudged American election—between two variants of cold war advocacy—and by four more years for President Reagan.

But the power of the armourers has been slipping at the edges. Denmark has refused contributions to cruise and Pershing. Holland has gained a muted victory for peace, in postponing the deployment decision, and Belgium is likely to follow. Greece continues to negotiate with her neighbours a

Balkan nuclear-free zone. In Spain the outcome of the long-delayed referendum on NATO still hangs in the balance. Not only Romania but also, it seems clear, Hungary and Bulgaria have been resisting Soviet military pressures. In New Zealand the incoming government has honoured its electoral pledges, proclaimed the islands to be nuclear-free, and is negotiating with neighbours a South Pacific nuclear-free zone. It is not true that 'nothing can be done'.

Yet these are only the visible signs of far deeper political transformations. We have lived with these for so long—we have ourselves *been* that transformation—that we have scarcely noticed what is going on. A first effect, in major Western nations, has been the polarisation of opinion; but a polarisation which at the same time has shattered beyond repair the all-party Atlanticist 'consensus' (excluding only certain Communist Parties) which had for thirty years legitimated not only every measure of armament but also the official management of opinion.

Of critical importance has been the detachment of major Western Social-Democratic Parties (West German, Danish, Dutch, Greek and the British Labour Party) from their automatic Atlanticist complicity. Around this there has been a much wider movement of opinion, ranging through Greens and smaller nationalist parties, churches, trade unions and professions, women's movements, and deeply into Liberal and (in some nations) Christian Democratic opinion.

At the same time the contest against particular weapons-systems (cruise and Pershing) passed by imperceptible stages into a contest by West European nations to regain their autonomy from United States hegemony. This has not been checked by the first deployments. For it is now evident that there are divergent European versus American national political objectives (notably, West German *ostpolitik* which is increasingly endorsed by substantial conservative interests) —divergencies accentuated by increasing competition between United States and West European economies, dramatically expressed by the interest-rates which have lifted the US dollar like a gas-balloon.

This cross-Atlantic tension is an enduring trend, and there

is no way in which the old kind of American military-diplomatic-economic hegemony can be reimposed on Western European nations. Paradoxically, now that NATO Chieftain Reagan (with his Tomahawks) has got his four more years this is bound to accelerate the disintegration of NATO in its old form, since Reagan is C-in-C of exactly those forces (military adventurers, merciless financiers, and illiterate amateur diplomats) who most provoke alarm among cautious West European elites. Lord Carrington, the incoming Secretary-General of NATO, is more flexible than the late, loud and unlamented Dr Joseph Luns. But, not for the first time, Carrington has taken the wrong job for the wrong boss at the wrong time. He will be kept busy as the aristocratic caretaker of a preserved bourgeois monument in a state of decay.

The NATO ruling groups won the great Euromissile contest. But the price of victory was almost as high as the price of defeat. They do not wish to re-enact the traumatic political contest of 1981–3. As Norman Birnbaum has written:

> While the peace movement did not block Euromissile deployment, that will be the last military decision imposed by NATO's technocrats: matters of arms, strategy and tactics are now subject to public scrutiny. The parties of the European centre and right have exhausted nearly all their political credit in enforcing the Euromissile decision, and European governments are increasingly at pains to avoid giving the impression of blind subservience to the United States.
>
> ('Europeanization of Europe', *Bulletin of the Atomic Scientists*, January 1985)

Kohl, Thatcher and Craxi are aware that alternative governments wait in the wings, which would depart from the forty-year-old Atlanticist norms. In 1984 they altered course from abrasive confrontation to little gestures of 'dialogue', borrowing the peace movement's own lines. Ministers scurry on visits to East European capitals, and (despite denials) a fragile 'second tier' of diplomacy is being erected between the superpowers. Symptoms of confusion and self-doubt are spreading within the European governing parties and the armed services themselves. These tensions have enforced upon the United States a return to the negotiating table. The Geneva talks are not being held because President Reagan has been born again in his second incarnation, and wishes to go down in the history books as a Man of Peace. They are not being held because the United States wishes to reach an agreement with the Russians. The talks are necessary to placate Western public opinion and to hold NATO together.

These tensions need not point in the direction of peace. Indeed, if it were not for the presence of the peace movement and its political allies, they could point to the resurgence of competing West European nationalisms, with the dominant statist and capitalist institutions (West German and French) working to create a new Euro-superpower, armed to the teeth with home-made provisions, both nuclear and conventional: Hades, Exocets, Mirages and Tornados. But the faction-fighting within NATO which will continue for several years will afford a significant political space within which peace forces can press for alternatives. These alternatives might include, but must go far beyond, scenarios for 'alternative defence'. They must be *political* alternatives, which envisage Rapacki-style diplomacies of reconciliation and mutual security between the nations of East and West Europe.

The refraction of the ideas of the peace movement, in their challenge to the premises of the Cold War, has penetrated every area of political and intellectual life. In Britain five years ago public discussion of matters of 'defence' was controlled within a supposed all-party 'consensus' which had endured for thirty years. I wrote in December 1979:

> The 'all-party consensus', and *especially* the submission of the Parliamentary Labour Party to the 'consensus', is the lynch-pin of the whole operation. It is this fiction which legitimates all that is done to us—the suppression of information, the manipulation of the media, the exclusion of critical questions from the arena of national political life.
>
> (*Writing by Candlelight*, p. 271)

That lynch-pin has now been struck out and the matter of 'defence' has been thrown open to the nation's debate. If the debate was not won in the unfavourable terms of the General Election of 1983, yet it is worth recalling that about one-third of the electorate then voted for parties supporting policies which, in the previous seven or eight general elections, had not even been on offer as serious options. That is not a bad beginning.

There are other consequences of this collapse of the fiction of consensus. It is more difficult to manage the broadcasting media in the old 'consensual' ways (although it should be made much more difficult than it is), while civil servants become increasingly resentful at being forced to undertake, in the name of 'national security', partisan party-political tasks of misinforming the public and of concealing information from parliament. The Sarah Tisdall and Clive Ponting cases may be leading us to a crisis of confidence within the public service, which can be resolved in only two ways. Either we must have a repeal of the Official Secrets Acts, new measures for Freedom of Information, and new forms of public accountability over military and security operations. Or Mrs Thatcher will arm the authoritarian security state with even more draconic powers.

Our balance-sheet of the past five years gives unexpected results. The massive international disarmament movement has, in the past years, achieved no measures of disarmament. Nor does it seem likely to achieve any, not even a qualified 'freeze', in the immediate future. But the implosion of the peace movement has achieved extraordinary results in the spheres of politics and of general consciousness. We have stripped the veils of consensus from our nuclear predicament and made it visible to all; our movements have precipitated the crystallisation of new political forms and alliances; they have made visible not only the weapons but also the premises of the Cold War. There is a paradox here. For our movements have acquired a reasonable expertise as disarmers, while we have remained puerile as politicians. Yet our successes have been registered where our expertise is least.

What conclusions should we draw from this? First, we

must accept and welcome this enlarged political agenda. A peace movement must engage with the 'national security' state (in West or East); must attend to its alliances in the Third World; and cannot avoid engagement with the problems of bloc division.

The threat of war does not rest upon weapons-systems alone, as if these were some kind of self-generating automata; it rests also upon political and ideological confrontation. The Cold War stands upon two legs: a permanent war economy and a permanent enemy hypothesis. Of the two, it may turn out that it is the ideological leg which is the more brittle; and the one which the peace movement, as a movement of ideas and popular energies, is best equipped to overthrow.

It is the permanent enemy hypothesis ('What about the Russians?') which has held in check the peace movement. The animating spirit of modern statism—on both sides of the Cold War—exists in this hypothesis: in some worst-case analysis the Other *might* be an enemy, or would be an enemy if it were not for nuclear 'deterrence'. It is normal in times of war for states to acquire emergency powers. What distinguishes the Cold War era is that the hypothesis of 'emergency' is built into the daily routines of the peacetime state. This supplies, for the authority of the modern state, what the hypothesis of Satan supplied for the medieval church. It is the need for 'defence' against a worst-case hypothesis which legitimates the paramountcy of 'national security' in whose name the Moscow Trust Group is harassed, and the employees at GCHQ Cheltenham are despoiled of their trade union rights.

The permanent enemy hypothesis is the most jealously-guarded component of ideology on both sides of the Cold War since it is highly functional for the governing elites. They would not know how to govern without it. It is necessary for there to be an enemy in order to keep client states in control. It is an ever-present means of internal ideological and social control. This keeps the security organs on constant alert, and can be used to lampoon peace movements in the West and civil rights movements in the East as potential traitors or auxiliaries of the Other.

Even more alarming, the permanent enemy hypothesis has come to serve, for the vast and variously-assembled populations of the two superpowers as a surrogate nationalism. Not for the first time, Middle America has been 'walking tall' and chanting 'four more years' in a spurious nationalist fervour whose fiction is that America is not a nation at all but is 'the Future' or 'the Free World'—a nationalism which defines its identity in 'standing up to the Commies' in Grenada, Nicaragua or the Soviet Union.

Reagan has won in the polls because he knows how to massage this enlarged and braggart nationalist ego. And if dismal recent reports are to be trusted, there is now an authentic surge of nationalist feeling in the Soviet Union also, whose citizens are constantly told that they find their identity as custodians of 'the heartland of Socialism' threatened by imperialist warmongers—a mood neither so brash nor so aggressive as the American mood, but nevertheless xenophobic (there are new penalties for hosting foreigners in Soviet homes) and introverted. Not for the first time, Russia is turning in upon herself. As a new succession crisis develops, there is evidence of the old siege mentality in which the entire political and cultural world is viewed in Manichean terms. The battle rages between Soviet light and imperialist darkness, and any intermediate tone or third way is instantly exposed as a cunning NATO trap.

These ideological forces are as threatening to peace as are any nuclear missiles, and there is no way in which a serious peace movement can keep them off the agenda. How, then, is the permanent enemy hypothesis to be confronted, when the ideologists and politicians of both sides are doing their best to confirm their enemy status with every move? It is no good offering a flat denial: 'the Russians (or the Americans) aren't coming.' The Russians are already there, as unwelcome occupants of several East European countries and in the five-year old (and still unending) war in Afghanistan. The Americans are already there, based across the globe, and they may well be coming, to Nicaragua or Cuba or the Middle East. And if we are right to show that the scenarios of Russian hordes sweeping down on the Channel Ports are implausible or absurd, nevertheless it is in the nature of a worst-case hypothesis that it will flicker in the popular imagination and can never finally be disproved.

The only way to contest the worst case is to envisage a better case, and then to summon up all our forces to work to bring that better case about. We cannot 'prove' this better case: it is the business of the peace movement to place it on the agenda, as historical possibility. And this is why the European peace movements occupy a space of peculiar opportunity and responsibility: opportunity because the unique political conditions of Europe, at this sensitive interface between the blocs, present to us a possible better case in which a healing and mediating process might commence on this continent: responsibility, because our duties to the Third World and to peace forces in the USA and USSR will best be met, not by ineffectual moralising about superpower sins, but by resolving our own political problems—that is, by disengaging Europe from the Cold War polarities and by strengthening the political and economic resources of the non-aligned world.

The opportunity is presented to us because those very forces which are exacerbating the tension between the superpowers are making Europe more vulnerable, provoking increasing opposition among the public of both halves, and forcing the question of greater autonomy upon the agenda. And here also the peace movement of the past five years has been a significant precipitate.

This may yet prove to be as important as any part of our work in the past five years. Beneath the carapace of censorship, East and Central Europe are now seething with debate, to which our voices have made some contribution. The dialogue now comes through to us in searching individual voices or from groups which signal a fellowship in our common cause. As discussion develops it becomes evident that there is as wide a plurality of opinions and perspectives in the East as in the West. And it is evident that even at the level of nation-states, there are diverging objectives and pressures for greater autonomy (Romania's truculence, Hungary's quiet and cautious 'westpolitik', Honecker's frustrated attempts at the same) which are analogous to the pressures away from superpower dominance in the West. As the Kremlin's succession-crisis drags on (a crisis which may have a bearing on the same issues), making Soviet policy by turns inert and capricious, the pressures for autonomy will grow.

We should not for a moment undervalue the importance of messages addressed to the Western peace movement from such influential organisations as Charter 77 and KOS. They are the sign that the old ideological compulsions of the Cold War which have at times divided the forces of the future from each other—peace as 'pro-Soviet', human rights as 'pro-American'—are breaking down. 'Peace' and 'liberty' are searching for convergent strategies.

Yet in my own view, at this moment, the growth of this dialogue, drawing in more voices and more sections of the public, is its own sufficient objective. There are thirty years of misrecognitions and suspicions to be worked through. The aim must for the time being be convergence and not identity.

To be effective, the dialogue between East and West must engage widening constituencies of citizens. It must not be co-opted by official diplomatic organs, and it must not be short-circuited into a few advanced intellectual groups. It must involve majority peace movements from the West, must be plural, and it cannot exclude the 'officials' of the East.

The issue here is not whether one talks with the 'officials' but how one talks and what one talks about? It is inevitable that there will be some abrasive exchanges. But we should refuse to be diverted into ideological generalities. We should demand the exchange and circulation among the publics of both sides of our policies and publications; rights and facilities of communication with any citizens on matters of peace; the opportunity for peace activists to visit each others' countries, to hold public and open workshops, seminars and lectures, and to meet with whom they please;

and guarantees that peace workers (whether in good or ill standing with the authorities) will not be harassed. That is an attainable minimum programme for dialogue, which cannot be dismissed as a 'provocation'.

If the ideologues of the World Peace Council have become confrontational, and are seeking to divide the Western peace movements, it does not help if radical sections of the Western movement become confrontational in return. We should not waste efforts investing, with drums and moral dramas, the castles of neo-Stalinist ideology; we should move around these and explore every road of dialogue, leaving their self-righteous custodians to starve in our rear. Forty years of complex interactive history cannot be reduced to a moment at its origin ('Yalta'); to heal that fracture in human polity and culture will require multiple initiatives of a kind far broader than accepted notions of 'politics'. And, in my own understanding, it is not moralistic dramas that the most hard-pressed of our independent friends in the East are asking for. Western radicals, in a half-open society, are accustomed to an abrasive style, to forcing open argument by challenge, confrontation and polemic. We understand too little the more subtle and silent pressures within the closed societies on the other side, which may work towards a similar convergence by less advertised means. For the sake of a self-righteous exercise in confrontation, we in the West may inflict real damage on friends in the East, forcing unnecessary polarisations upon them, and turning back the quiet tides of cultural convergence.

Moreover, if we are serious about the perspective of a historic compromise between the blocs, commencing in Europe—a perspective which would include nuclear-free zones, Rapacki-style diplomacies, bi-lateral agreements between nations East and West, the opening of frontiers to all kinds of travel and communications, mutual security agreements, the progressive 'Finlandisation' of Eastern Europe and 'Swedenisation' of Western Europe, and which might culminate in the mutual withdrawal of all American and Soviet forces from both halves of Europe—if we are serious about this, then these are processes which may be initiated by movements from below but must, in the end, be registered by the institutions of states. At some point in the future, under a new US President and a new First Secretary of the CPSU, there must be Summit meetings and conferences of European nations. Should we not be searching out the doves (or the realists) within the bureaucracies of both blocs now?

In conclusion I must make one matter absolutely clear. I have entered into argument, in these pages, with opponents of the peace movement, and have followed them into their own premises of political 'realism'. I make no apology for this. The peace movement is not just one of moral 'protest'. It exists to act in the real world, and to act with effect. We must propose our own historical agenda, and this must commence from the world as it is. The agenda which I have sketched is not one in which individuals—or single nations—can opt out of that world. It proposes a complex reciprocal process, in which the peace movement is an effective political agent, pressing forward and monitoring the transition to a healed human world.

But if it is to succeed in this, it must arouse everywhere a new kind of peace consciousness, founded upon the human ecological imperative of neighbourly survival. This means that it is right to found its position on an absolute: the refusal of nuclear weapons. It cannot entangle itself in the vocabulary of 'perhaps' or 'if-they-will-we-will' or in the theology of deterrence theory. If this leads us to be accused by our opponents of one-sidedness or moralism, then let us be one-sided moralists. Only an unqualified and implacable refusal of the obscenity of nuclear weapons will be strong enough to break that system at one point or another: and once the system begins to be broken, anywhere, we must summon up an international response. *That* will be the point at which all the politics in these pages will come in.

Nothing enforces this more clearly than the insanity into which the United States is now leading the world. Not even Jonathan Swift could have imagined so savage a satire on human endeavour as Star Wars. For what is the case with this? It is proposed that, in some 25 years, after the expenditure of several trillion dollars, United States technology will emerge with an impenetrable anti-ballistic missile shield. It has even been proposed, by President Reagan in a rhetorical aside, that at this point the United States will reveal all its technology to the USSR, although it is not yet certain that Reagan will still be President in 25 years time. (If he could circumvent the US Constitution he might still have some difficulty with his own.) So that it is proposed that, at astronomic cost, an astral venture will be set in motion (a venture which leading scientists and strategists have stated to be impossible) in order to achieve an end—the blocking of each others' missiles—which could be achieved tomorrow, at no cost at all, by a rational agreement by both to disarm.

When a palpable insanity grips national leaders it is necessary to probe the matter a little further. Nations do not normally lay heavy burdens on their tax-payers and inflate the national debt just to humour the fantasies of a leader—even one just born-again by ballot. We may suppose some hidden agenda or some ideological delirium here. In this case I detect both. The hidden agenda is supplied, of course, by the 'alchemists of the laboratories' and the very powerful arms manufacturing lobby, whose lips are drooling with the prospects of full order-books twenty and thirty years ahead. But even this powerful lobby, which is not yet a majority shareholder in the United States economy, could not trick the state and the public into a manifest insanity if there was not some even more powerful ulterior political drive.

Star Wars is the ultimate decomposition of deterrence theory, and the attempt by United States nuclear ideologists to return to the womb of Hiroshima. Ever since the Soviet Union reached forward to nuclear 'parity' they have become increasingly fretful. They possessed this huge bludgeoning and blackmailing power—which, however, could never be used, and, even worse, the world was beginning to tumble to this fact.* For a decade they have been trying out this

* See Alan Wolfe's wise comments, 'American Democracy and Nuclear Weapons', *World Policy Journal*, Fall 1984.

and that trick to regain nuclear 'superiority', but all were implausible. Then they tried scenarios of 'limited' nuclear war, on the territory of allies and other nations, but these have proved implausible also. Delving back in their memories, President Reagan and his friends recalled those blissful five years, from 1945–50, when the United States had the Bomb and the Other did not. It is out of that frustration, and that delirium of ideology, that Star Wars was born. Let us abolish the Other's Bomb! Let us arm the moral ends of America with an impermeable shield! Let us once again be able to threaten a world which cannot threaten us! Once the solution was found (out of pure ideology) then money and know-how *must* be able to bring it about.

It is an ideological delirium which vibrates all the chords of the worst traditions of American right-wing populism. With astonishing simplicity it combines isolationism (they can't get us) with external menace. It combines the citizen's faith that whatever America does must be moral—and that the Bomb is God's gift to protect the 'Free World'—with the old American preference for 'fixing things' by technological means rather than by political resolutions. It massages the American ego by intoning homilies about 'saving humanity', while drawing humanity within new dimensions of danger.

We should not dismiss this as mere politician-talk, as cynical rhetoric to cover more limited objectives. Star Wars, with its space-fic glitter, encodes ideological forces which act in their own right. The President may himself be a true believer.

To find the most powerful nation on the earth to be crawling back into an ideological womb is a sign that the whole era of deterrence theory has at length come to an end. But it is a terrifying signal of our human predicament. This combination of material avarice (the arms lobby) and of ideological self-delusion is the apt terminus to my essay on 'Exterminism', written five years ago.

It is because the minds of our rulers are unhinged, and chaos has moved closer to us so that it chills the future's breath, that I affirm once again the imperative of refusal. The much-abused 'unilateralists', the campers at Greenham or Comiso, the demonstrators at the Livermore Laboratories, the harassed Moscow Trust Group, the 'Swords into Ploughshare' youth—they may not have got every argument right, but they affirm the one essential argument upon which our survival depends. There can be no technological shield against nuclear evil. There is—and there has been for forty years—only one shield against chaos: that pitifully weak and yet somehow indestructable shield, the human conscience. In the past five years that shield has become international. It is the peace movement. I salute its work.